THEORY INTO PRACTICE

Summer 2006 • Volume 45, Number 3

This Issue: Inclusive Schooling Practices: From Why to How	205
The Role of 1:1 Individual Instruction in Reading *Nancy Frey*	207
Modifying Schoolwork in Inclusive Classrooms *Rachel E. Janney and Martha E. Snell*	215
Peer Supports and Inclusive Education: An Underutilized Resource *Rebecca Bond and Elizabeth Castagnera*	224
Teachers as Executives *Nancy K. French and Ritu V. Chopra*	230
The Many Faces of Collaborative Planning and Teaching *Jacqueline S. Thousand, Richard A. Villa, and Ann I. Nevin*	239
Assessment of Progress in the General Curriculum for Students With Disabilities *Diane M. Browder, Shawnee Y. Wakeman, and Claudia Flowers*	249
Inclusion as Social Justice: Critical Notes on Discourses, Assumptions, and the Road Ahead *Alfredo J. Artiles, Nancy Harris-Murri, and Dalia Rostenberg*	260
Comprehensive School Reform and Inclusive Schools *James McLeskey and Nancy L. Waldron*	269
Promoting Systemic, Statewide Inclusion From the Bottom Up *Virginia Roach and Christine Salisbury*	279
Additional Resources for Classroom Use	287

Guest Editor: Douglas Fisher

This Issue

How different will it be when children who understand and celebrate individual differences run the world?

THAT SIMPLE QUESTION has guided much of my work in inclusive schools. I would like to be part of a world where individual differences are respected, valued, and celebrated. As such, we must learn to ask ourselves, each day, what we have done to ensure that public school students understand the diversity they will experience as adults.

Part of the answer to this question comes in the form of inclusive education. Inclusive education provides opportunities for students with disabilities to acquire skills, enhance their communication, and make friends (Fisher, Roach, & Frey, 2002). Inclusive education also ensures that students without disabilities experience and appreciate at least one form of diversity (Staub & Peck, 1995). What then do I mean by inclusive education? Generally, inclusive education means that students with disabilities attend their home school with their age and grade peers and are educated in regular classes with appropriate supports and services. Related services, such as speech or physical therapy, are provided within the context of the general education class, rather than being offered in the more traditional pull-out model.

Students continue to address individualized education plan goals, but skills and objectives are infused within the curriculum everyone else uses. For instance, measurement skills can be practiced within a science-lab, and communication goals can be acquired during world history class. Inclusive education also means more broadly defining how students can demonstrate their mastery of content. Examples include the student completing a shorter assignment, using assistive technology to access a specific activity, or creating a three-dimensional project versus a term paper. Thus, special education becomes a series of supports and services that can be provided in a variety of general education settings instead of it being defined as a specific placement.

Collaboration among general and special education teachers—as well as support from administrators, families, and community members—is essential for schools to become inclusive. Teachers and parents have conceptualized the supports and services that all students use. Effective inclusive education is articulated through the organization of personal supports, curriculum supports, behavioral supports, and technology supports. For example, personal supports may involve special education teachers, paraprofessionals, or peers providing in-class supports such as oral tests, note-taking, or redirection. Curriculum accommodations and modifications allow students to access interesting and exciting general education activities that are challenging but not frustrating. Instructional and assistive technology ranges from computers to speech output devices to pencil grips.

Educators and parents today generally acknowledge that students with disabilities must access the general education curriculum in the regular classroom if we are to ensure that no child is left behind. The real issue today is how to make inclusive schooling a reality for students.

A decade ago, *Theory Into Practice* published an issue on inclusive schooling entitled "Inclusive Schools: The Continuing Debate." The articles significantly influenced the field and helped to facilitate the conversation about inclusive education and why this change in the service delivery system was necessary. As the guest editors noted, "this issue focuses on the emerging, new relationship between general education and special education" (Paul & Cartledge, 1996, p. 2). The articles argued the *why* question—why should students with disabilities be educated in the regular classroom?

This issue of *Theory Into Practice* reflects the evolution of the field. As a profession, we are now asking *how* more often than *why* in regard to inclusive schooling. The authors in this issue explore the range of supports and structures that must be in place to ensure that all students become successful, contributing members of the community. The topics we discuss today center on literacy for all students (Frey), modifying schoolwork (Janney & Snell), the role of peers and paraprofessionals (Bond & Castagnera; French & Chopra), collaboration between general and special educators (Thousand, Villa, & Nevin), access to curriculum and assessment systems (Browder, Wakeman, & Flowers), how inclusive schooling relates to social justice (Artiles, Murri, & Rostenberg), and systems change at the whole school (McLeskey & Waldron) and state level (Roach & Salisbury). I concur with the vision for inclusive schools established by Paul and Cartledge (1996), "to provide an interpretation that will inspire others to conduct further theoretical, research, and critical investigations on a topic important for both general and special educators and, ultimately, for all children in educational settings" (p. 3). And I hope that this issue contributes to that purpose. I also hope that this issue pushes the world forward just a quarter of an inch. If we each were to push the world forward that little bit, imagine how close we would be to changing the world.

References

Fisher, D., Roach, V., & Frey, N. (2002). Examining the general programmatic benefits on inclusive schools. *International Journal of Inclusive Education, 6,* 63–78.

Paul, P., & Cartledge, G. (1996). This issue. *Theory Into Practice, 35,* 2–3.

Staub, D., & Peck, C. A. (1995). What are the outcomes for nondisabled students? *Educational Leadership, 52*(4), 36–40.

Guest Editor
Douglas Fisher
San Diego State University

Nancy Frey

The Role of 1:1 Individual Instruction in Reading

General education classrooms are increasingly diverse as students with and without disabilities learn alongside one another. At each level, all students are learning to read and reading to learn standards-based content. A worry among some general and special educators who otherwise support the principles of inclusive education is what to do about the differences in academic levels between students with and without disabilities. This question is raised frequently in regard to reading instruction. This article makes a case for the use of 1:1 instruction that is often delivered in the general education classroom as a model for providing students with disabilities with access to specialized assistance.

ANDREW SETTLES INTO A CHAIR in a quiet area of his second-grade classroom. Ms. Matthews, a special educator, welcomes him and begins a guided reading lesson using the book

---

Nancy Frey is an Associate Professor in the School of Teacher Education at San Diego State University.

Correspondence should be addressed to Nancy Frey, School of Teacher Education, San Diego State University, 5500 Campanile Drive, San Diego, CA 92105. E-mail: nfrey@mail.sdsu.edu.

Snowy Gets a Wash (Randall, 1997). She will use this instructional time to introduce the story and the word families *-ake* and *-ide*. Ms. Matthews often preteaches the skills Andrew's classroom teacher will use later in the morning. For Andrew, access to 1:1 instruction provides him with the opportunity to preview activities.

Miriam meets with inclusion support facilitator Mr. Habib to review the key concepts on the moon, a topic just taught by her eighth-grade science teacher. Using a picture book text written at her reading level, Mr. Habib and Miriam read about the Earth's gravity in *Could We Live on the Moon?* (Wishinsky, 2005). For Miriam, access to 1:1 instruction means that she can review science concepts first introduced by her science teacher.

Hiroshi and the high school reading specialist meet twice a week in the 11th-grade American literature class. Students in his class are meeting in pairs to discuss the novels of Jack London. Ms. Santiago and Hiroshi read and discuss an illustrated version of *Call of the Wild* (London & Yamamoto, 2002). The reading specialist uses this time to provide direct instruction on reading comprehension strategies such as predicting, determining importance, summarizing, and evaluating. For Hiroshi, access to 1:1 instruction allows him to receive instruction on concepts not being taught in his general education classroom.

A Rationale for 1:1 Instruction in Reading

The instructional delivery model known as 1:1 is different from, although not contradictory to, individualized instruction. The latter is a foundational principle of special education that requires students with disabilities to receive instruction tailored to their learning needs and strengths. Individualized instruction can be delivered in small groups or 1:1. Small group arrangements are more prevalent, commonly seen in pull-out resource programs and in the ability-grouping practices of general education classrooms. However, 1:1 instruction is rarely seen in general education classrooms and is often viewed as something that can be done only in a nonclassroom setting.

Inclusive education has evolved from the socialization goals of the 1980s to a focus on access to curriculum and standards-based instruction today. However, there is a danger that the increased emphasis on academic progress can have a backlash effect on these efforts. As the progress of students with disabilities has become a key measure in the accountability formulas of the nation's schools, there has been a retreat to segregated education in some places (Furney, Hasazi, Keefe, & Hartnett, 2003), especially among students who are culturally and linguistically diverse (Klingner et al., 2005). As literacy is viewed as crucial to academic achievement for all students, it is time to revisit 1:1 instruction as a tool in a comprehensive support plan for students with disabilities.

Effectiveness of 1:1 Instruction in Reading

The practice of a knowledgeable adult offering reading instruction to an individual student has been a valued approach in American education, although many teachers state that they rarely have time to do so (Moody, Vaughn, & Schumm, 1997). For students without disabilities, this is often accomplished through any number of reading intervention programs, such as Reading Recovery (Clay, 1993), Success for All (Madden, Slavin, Karweit, Dolan, & Wasik, 1993), and Early Steps (Santa & Hoien, 1999). These programs vary quite a bit from one another in terms of methodology and philosophy, but all share a belief in 1:1 instruction as an important component for ensuring student success. For example, Reading Recovery is a 30-min daily program for first graders delivered by highly trained program teachers. In contrast, Success for All is a schoolwide program that uses 20-min structured lessons with trained tutors. Early Steps, unlike the other two, is implemented by the child's classroom teacher.

There are, of course, many other 1:1 reading programs besides those mentioned. A meta-analysis of 31 studies of 1:1 reading tutoring programs found that "well-designed, reliably implemented, 1:1 interventions can make significant contributions to improved reading outcomes for many students whose poor reading skills place them at risk for academic failure" (Elbaum, Vaughn, Hughes, & Moody, 2000, p. 617). This finding is consistent with a similar study of five 1:1 reading programs from earlier in the decade (Wasik & Slavin, 1993).

Like general education, the special education field has a long history of 1:1 instruction. As the field has evolved over the last decades of the 20th century, so has the role of individual instruction for students with disabilities. At one time, 1:1 instruction was emblematic of special education, especially for students with more significant disabilities (Winzer, 1993). However, as the knowledge base of the field has deepened, the time and place for individual instruction has been problematic.

History of 1:1 Instruction in Special Education

One-to-one instruction first rose to prominence in institutional settings. Institutionalized schools specializing in specific types of disabilities such as visual or hearing impairments were established in the 19th century, and although education was seen as a secondary goal (after issues of safety and comfort), instruction was often performed individually (Winzer, 1993). By the early 20th century, some students with disabilities were attending clustered and segregated day classes organized by age, intelligence testing, or shared subfeatures of the disability (Wright & Anne, 1988).

One intended goal was that by clustering students according to learning or behavioral characteristics, the more expensive 1:1 instruction would be unnecessary. Such classrooms depended on the efficiency of whole group instruction to advance student learning. Segregated practices were seen as a way to concentrate resources for the benefit of students and the convenience of the adults who taught them.

As the emerging field of special education codified in the decades of the 1960s and 1970s, several instructional practices became firmly associated with the discipline. In particular, training in language and behavioral processes became a feature of the special education classroom (Polloway, 2002). Remediation became the goal, as illustrated by psycholinguistics training for language-based disabilities (Kirk & Bateman, 1962). McLeskey (2004) explains that these

> "process training" methods were built on the idea that (a) components of student language are identifiable and measurable, (b) these components provide the underpinning for learning, and (c) if the components were defective, they could be remediated. It was assumed that once this remediation occurred, the student's classroom learning would improve. (p. 82)

One-to-one instruction enjoyed a renewed status as it came to be viewed as a means for achieving this remediation.

Students with more significant disabilities were also taught using principles of training and remediation. The behavior modification approach, with its repeated trials and token reward system, soon became a staple of most special education classrooms (O'Leary & Becker, 1967). Although psycholinguistics training and behavior modification were later found to be ineffective, the structure of repeated trials using a 1:1 teacher/student ratio as a principle was firmly ingrained in special education classrooms.

The Dissonance Between Principle and Reality

However, the issue of access to specialized instruction in special education classrooms remained problematic. Despite the promise of special education classrooms as a place to benefit from 1:1 instruction, the reality was that these classrooms rarely offered the opportunity to provide such services. Vaughn, Moody, and Schumm (1998) called this dissonance a *broken promise* because when it did occur in the 14 classrooms they observed over a school year, it was seldom sustained for any significant length of time—usually less than 1 min. The researchers attributed these findings to several factors, including beliefs by some special education teachers that individual instruction was harmful to the self-esteem of students. In addition, many of the participants found the number of students and the range of needs to be overwhelming. Therefore, whole class instruction was perceived as a more efficient means for teaching, even though students failed to achieve (Vaughn et al., 1998).

Their findings corroborated those of Allington and McGill-Franzen a decade earlier (1989), in which the reading instruction of 64 students in Grades 2, 4, and 8 were observed in general education classrooms, Chapter 1 pull-out programs, and special education classrooms. The researchers found that students in the special education classrooms received only 25% of the instructional time devoted to reading that their peers in general education received (1,333 observed min vs. 4,233). Moreover, active teaching consumed only 37% (492 min) of instructional time in the special education classroom, with the remainder devoted to seat work or other nonreading activities (Allington & McGill-Franzen, 1989). They noted that "time spent in seat work activities is not a potent predictor of reading achievement" (p. 538). As the 1980s drew to a close, special educators began to advocate for increased access to general education (Will, 1986).

Nevertheless, the physical relocation of students with disabilities into general education classrooms did not make these issues disappear. Critics of inclusive practices have reported that general education teachers who taught students with disabilities did not differentiate instruction or teach using a variety of grouping strategies (Baker & Zigmond, 1990). These and other researchers have attributed this in part to an expectation that students with disabilities needed to conform to the demands of the general education classroom (e.g., Gersten, Walker, & Darch, 1988).

This may have less to do with students with disabilities specifically and more to do with resistance to any deviation from the practice of *teaching to the middle*. For example, similar findings have occurred in studies regarding students identified as gifted (Reis, Grubbins, & Briggs, 2004), low achieving (Thompson, Warren, & Carter, 2004), and English language learners (Olivio, 2003). In spite of these phenomena, few have called for the removal of these students from the general education classroom. To the contrary, the profession continues to advocate for better teaching practices to meet the needs of individual learners. Resistance to differentiation of instruction may be a product of a lack of teacher knowledge (Frey & Fisher, 2004).

The Nexus Between General and Special Education

What is clear is that general and special education have something to offer students with disabilities. The field of special education is moving away from its one-dimensional designation as a place, and increasingly defines itself as a continuum of services and supports. General education is recognizing that students with individualized education plans are not someone else's students. An important goal of special education in the 21st century is to identify and refine sound instructional practices that use the best of special and general education. This nexus represents the current and future direction of education for students with disabilities.

Special education has developed "a legacy of enduring practices, including individualized instruction" (Mostert & Crockett, 2000, p. 139) and it is prudent to incorporate these enduring practices within the context of inclusive education. As well, general education offers standards-based curriculum and the power of peers as language, academic, and social models (Freeman & Alkin, 2000; Kennedy, Shukla, & Fryxell, 1997). Rather than viewing 1:1 instruction as an either/or proposition, today's inclusive classrooms use this approach as part of a system of supports and services. However, the use of 1:1 instruction should be based on three principles:

- One-to-one instruction is appropriate for a wide range of students.
- One-to-one instruction is one part of a comprehensive education.
- One-to-one instruction complements classroom instruction.

Appropriateness for a Wide Range of Students

Special education has moved beyond the naïve practice of equating support needs with the specific disability. For instance, we know that a student with a learning disability may need behavioral supports, or that a learner with a cognitive disability may also require a modification to the physical environment to ensure access. As well, the decision to use 1:1 instruction should be predicated on the needs of the student, not on the label. Andrew, the student with a learning disability in the opening scenario, uses 1:1 instruction to preview reading material his classroom teacher will soon teach in more detail. His special educator, Ms. Matthews, meets with Andrew about once a week to preview his reading instruction with him. On the other hand, the reading specialist sees Hiroshi, a student with a cognitive disability, at regularly scheduled intervals to work on his reading skills. Access to 1:1 instruction that complements the instruction of the general education classroom is an effective means for increasing the literacy skills of students with significant disabilities (Ryndak, Morrison, & Sommerstein, 1999). Likewise, not every student with a disability needs 1:1 instruction. It should be used judiciously, as with all potential accommodations and modifications.

Savage and Armstrong (2003) advise that the purposes of individual instruction fall into four categories: rate, content, method of presentation, and goals. These variables can be used to determine how often and to what extent a student needs 1:1 instruction. For instance, is the purpose to address the rate of learning, as in Andrew's case? Or does the student need content instruction not currently offered by the general education curriculum, as with Hiroshi? A clear understanding of the purposes for 1:1 instruction can prevent misunderstandings between general and special educators.

One Part of a Comprehensive Education

An effective classroom offers a variety of learning experiences delivered through a variety of instructional formats. These formats include limited amounts of whole group focus lessons for modeling and scaffolding skills and strategies, guided instruction for coaching, collaborative learning to tap into the power of peers, and independent work for mastery (Frey & Fisher, 2006). Therefore, 1:1 guided instruction is situated within the context of a comprehensive education available to all students.

Like all lessons, 1:1 instruction requires planning to make the most of instructional time. This prevents the session from devolving into a less pedagogically rigorous lesson that focuses on helping rather than teaching. The same principles that apply to effective group teaching apply to the individual lesson: activation of background knowledge, introduction of concepts and vocabulary, and student demonstration of learning (Good & Brophy, 2003). Consider each of these guiding questions to facilitate individual lesson planning:

1. What is the purpose of the lesson? One-to-one lessons can be conducted to match the *rate of learning* for the student, such as previewing skills or providing more opportunities for guided practice. Others may benefit from *content instruction*, especially to build factual or conceptual knowledge necessary to participate in other classroom activities. Some students with disabilities may require an alternative *method of presentation,* as Miriam did when she worked with Mr. Habib using a science picture book written at a different grade level. Finally, 1:1 lessons may be conducted to teach alternative *learning goals* that are not being taught to the other members of the class.
2. What are the student's background knowledge and prior experiences? Effective teachers use the learner's prior experiences and background knowledge to build new understanding (Bransford, Brown, & Cocking, 2000). When planning the lesson, consider what academic and life experiences a student has had, as well as the background knowledge he or she possesses. When Mr. Habib began his lesson with Miriam, he used some of the equipment from the science teacher's gravity demonstration to review concepts.
3. What are the targeted skills or strategies for this lesson? It is critical to not only be exact in what will be taught but to also communicate it to the learner. One-to-one instruction is academically intense and often lasts 20 min or so. Therefore, it is important to resist the urge to cram too many skills or strategies into one session, as this can be confusing (and exhausting) for the student. It is better to focus on specific concepts or skills, teach them, and then return the student to the flow of classroom activities. One-to-one instruction is about precision.
4. How will essential vocabulary be taught? Individual instruction is an ideal time for introducing or practicing academic vocabulary. A few minutes of instruction and discussion is useful for expanding vocabulary, the best predictor for academic success (Espin & Foegen, 1996). The opportunities for oral language development in 1:1 instruction should not be overlooked. This is an ideal time for the learner to have multiple occasions to use the target vocabulary orally, in writing, or with a speech output device. Ms. Matthews made sure that Andrew understood the meanings as well as the graphophonic relationships of the word families.
5. What will the student write or produce? A measure of effectiveness of any lesson is the assessment of learning. Evidence of learning can take a multitude of forms, including oral, written, and performance products. For example, after Andrew was taught about the word families, Ms. Matthews gave him a closed-word sort to complete (Gillet & Temple, 1978). As she observed, Andrew placed

the *-ake* and *-ide* words written on 3 × 5 cards into the correct piles.
6. What future skills will the student need? This is perhaps the most critical part of 1:1 instruction because a goal is to integrate classroom instruction as much as possible. This reflective feedback is critical to the communication between special and general educators.

A planning form for developing a 1:1 instructional lesson should address each of the previous questions. In addition to planning, it can also serve as a way to document the specialized services provided for the student.

Complementing Classroom Instruction

A long-held principle of special education is that the learning milieu is altered as minimally as possible while still ensuring meaningful participation—summarized in the catchphrase *only as special as necessary*. The general education classroom is the context within which all decisions about accommodations or modifications are designed (Janney & Snell, 2004). Thus the teaching done during 1:1 instruction complements and supplements classroom instruction but does not replace it. Like other instructional arrangements (whole group, small group, and partners), individual instruction is a grouping format used as needed to support continued learning (Flood, Lapp, Flood, & Nagel, 1992). It does not become the primary vehicle for delivering instruction in isolation from the rest of the classroom.

As noted earlier, the field of special education has advanced since its inception. Decades of institutions, schools, and classrooms for students with disabilities have demonstrated that the practice of segregation does not lead to anything other than segregated adult outcomes (Blackorby & Wagner, 1996; Dunn, 1968; Hasazi, Gordon, & Roe, 1985). Therefore the use of 1:1 reading instruction should not be viewed as a retreat from the growth in the knowledge base of the field. As with other decisions for students with disabilities, the general education classroom must be considered first. In nearly all cases, 1:1 instruction can be delivered in the classroom, not in a separate physical location. Depending on the learner and the classroom, it may be offered at the student's desk or in a quieter location in the room. The goal should be to minimize time lost to transition, such as relocating to another setting. Most important, 1:1 instruction offered in the classroom connotes a powerful set of values: this learner is a member of this classroom, not a visitor who "comes and goes" (Schnorr, 1990, p. 231).

Conclusion

One-to-one reading instruction is a useful practice to support some students with disabilities in the general education classroom. Although not necessary for all, it can be useful for students who benefit from a change of the rate, content, method of presentation, or alternative academic goals. The use of 1:1 instruction should be viewed as part of a comprehensive educational experience that involves a variety of learning experiences, including whole group, small group, and peer partners. It is never intended to replace the instruction occurring in the general education classroom.

As special education has evolved from segregated to inclusive practices, it is vital to retain what we have learned along the way. Inclusive education, and the general and special educators who are vital to its success, bring a host of talents and a knowledge base with them to the classroom. One-to-one instruction is one tool for capitalizing on the best of both worlds.

References

Allington, R. L., & McGill-Franzen, A. (1989). School response to reading failure: Instruction for Chapter I and special education students in grades two, four, and eight. *Elementary School Journal, 89,* 529–542.

Baker, J. M., & Zigmond, N. (1990). Are regular education classes equipped to accommodate students with learning disabilities? *Exceptional Children, 56,* 515–526.

Blackorby, J., & Wagner, M. (1996). Longitudinal postschool outcomes of youth with disabilities:

Findings from the National Longitudinal Transition Study. *Exceptional Children, 62,* 399–413.

Bransford, J. L., Brown, A. L., & Cocking, R. R. (Eds.). (2000). *How people learn: Brain, mind, experience, and school.* Washington, DC: National Academies Press.

Clay, M. M. (1993). *Reading recovery: A guidebook for teachers in training.* Portsmouth, NH: Heinemann.

Dunn, L. (1968). Special education for the mildly retarded: Is much of it justified? *Exceptional Children, 35,* 5–22.

Elbaum, B., Vaughn, S., Hughes, M. T., & Moody, S. (2000). How effective are one-to-one tutoring programs in reading for elementary students at risk for reading failure? A meta-analysis of the intervention research. *Journal of Educational Psychology, 92,* 605–619.

Espin, C. A., & Foegen, A. (1996). Validity of general outcome measures for predicting secondary students' performance on content-area tasks. *Exceptional Children, 62,* 497–514.

Flood, J., Lapp, D., Flood, S., & Nagel, G. (1992). Am I allowed to group? Using flexible grouping patterns for effective instruction. *The Reading Teacher, 45,* 608–618.

Freeman, S., & Alkin, M. (2000). Academic and social attainments for students with mental retardation in general education and special education classrooms. *Remedial and Special Education, 21,* 3–18.

Frey, N., & Fisher, D. (2004). School change and teacher knowledge: A reciprocal relationship. *Teacher Education and Special Education, 27,* 57–66.

Frey, N., & Fisher, D. (2006). *Language arts workshop: Purposeful reading and writing instruction.* Upper Saddle River, NJ: Prentice Hall.

Furney, K. S., Hasazi, S. B., Keefe, K. C., & Hartnett, J. (2003). A longitudinal analysis of shifting policy landscapes in special and general education reform. *Exceptional Children, 70,* 81–94.

Gersten, R., Walker, H., & Darch, C. (1988). Relationships between teachers' effectiveness and their tolerance for handicapped students. *Exceptional Children, 54,* 433–438.

Gillet, J. W., & Temple, C. (1978). Word knowledge: A cognitive view. *Reading World, 18,* 132–140.

Good, T. L., & Brophy, J. E. (2003). *Looking in classrooms* (9th ed.). Boston: Allyn & Bacon.

Hasazi, S., Gordon, L., & Roe, C. (1985). Factors associated with employment status of handicapped youth exiting high schools from 1979–1983. *Exceptional Children, 51,* 455–469.

Janney, R., & Snell, M. E. (2004). *Modifying schoolwork* (2nd ed.). Baltimore: Brookes.

Kennedy, C. H., Shukla, S., & Fryxell, D. (1997). Comparing the effects of educational placement on the social relationships of intermediate school students with severe disabilities. *Exceptional Children, 64,* 31–48.

Kirk, S., & Bateman, B. (1962). Diagnosis and remediation of learning disabilities. *Exceptional Children, 29,* 73–78.

Klingner, J. K., Artiles, A. J., Kozleski, E., Harry, B., Zion, S., Tate, W., et al. (2005). Addressing the disproportionate representation of culturally and linguistically diverse students in special education through culturally responsive systems. *Education Policy Analysis Archives, 13,* Article 38. Retrieved September 25, 2005, from http://epaa.asu.edu/epaa/v13n38/

London, J., & Yamamoto, M. (2002). *Call of the wild: Great illustrated classics.* Edina, MN: Abdo.

Madden, N. A., Slavin, R. E., Karweit, N. L., Dolan, L. J., & Wasik, B. A. (1993). Success for all: Longitudinal effects of a restructuring program for inner-city elementary schools. *American Educational Research Journal, 30,* 123–148.

McLeskey, J. (2004). Classic articles in special education: Articles that shaped the field, 1960–1996. *Remedial and Special Education, 25,* 79–87.

Moody, S. W., Vaughn, S., & Schumm, J. S. (1997). Instructional grouping for reading: Teachers' views. *Remedial and Special Education, 18,* 347–356.

Mostert, M. P., & Crockett, J. B. (2000). Reclaiming the history of special education for more effective practice. *Exceptionality, 8,* 133–143.

O'Leary, K., & Becker, W. (1967). Behavior modification of an adjustment class: A token reinforcement program. *Exceptional Children, 33,* 637–642.

Olivio, W. (2003). "Quit talking and learn English!": Conflicting language ideologies in an ESL classroom. *Anthropology and Education Quarterly, 34,* 50–71.

Polloway, E. A. (2002). The profession of learning disabilities: Progress and promises. *Learning Disability Quarterly, 25,* 103–112.

Randall, B. (1997). *Snowy gets a wash.* Crystal Lake, IL: Rigby.

Reis, M., Grubbins, E. J., & Briggs, C. J. (2004). Reading instruction for talented readers: Case studies documenting few opportunities for continuous progress. *Gifted Child Quarterly, 48,* 315–338.

Ryndak, D. L., Morrison, A., & Sommerstein, L. (1999). Literacy before and after inclusion: A case study. *Journal of the Association for Persons With Severe Handicaps, 24,* 5–22.

Santa, C., & Hoein, T. (1999). An assessment of early steps: A program for early intervention of reading problems. *Reading Research Quarterly, 34,* 54–73.

Savage, T. V., & Armstrong, D. G. (2003). *Effective teaching in elementary social studies* (5th ed.). Upper Saddle River, NJ: Prentice Hall.

Schnorr, R. T. (1990). "Peter? He comes and goes ... ": First graders' perspectives on a part-time mainstream student. *Journal of the Association for Persons With Severe Handicaps, 15,* 231–240.

Thompson, G. L., Warren, S., & Carter, L. (2004). It's not my fault: Predicting high school teachers who blame parents and students for students' low achievement. *The High School Journal, 87*(3), 5–14.

Vaughn, S., Moody, S., & Schumm, J. S. (1998). Broken promises: Reading instruction in the resource room. *Exceptional Children, 64,* 211–226.

Wasik, B. A., & Slavin, R. E. (1993). Preventing early reading failure with one-to-one tutoring: A review of five programs. *Reading Research Quarterly, 28,* 178–200.

Will, M. (1986). *Educating students with learning problems: A shared responsibility.* Washington, DC: U.S. Department of Education, Office of Special Education and Rehabilitation Services.

Winzer, M. (1993). *The history of special education: From isolation to integration.* Washington, DC: Gallaudet University Press.

Wishinsky, F. (2005). *Could we live on the moon?* Parsippany, NJ: Celebration.

Wright, D., & Anne, D. (1988). *From idiocy to mental deficiency: Historical perspectives on people with learning disabilities.* London: Routledge.

TiP

Rachel E. Janney
Martha E. Snell

Modifying Schoolwork in Inclusive Classrooms

This article focuses on the instructional aspects of inclusive education and describes how collaborating teams of general education and special education teachers can adapt instruction so that students with disabilities and their classmates without disabilities can learn together in shared activities. A model for creating individualized adaptations for the range of exceptional students encountered in inclusive schools is presented. The adaptations model is designed to facilitate the achievement of the goals of inclusive education by modifying schoolwork in the least intrusive way possible and ensuring social and instructional participation by students with disabilities. The steps of a process for designing curricular and instructional adaptations are summarized, and several planning tools to assist in making the process more efficient for teachers and more effective in enhancing student achievement and social belonging are described.

Rachel E. Janney is Professor of Special Education at Radford University. Martha E. Snell is Professor of Curriculum Instruction & Special Education at the University of Virginia.

Correspondence should be addressed to Rachel E. Janney, C156 Peters Hall, BOX 7006, Radford University, Radford, VA 24142. E-mail: rjanney@radford.edu

THE GOALS OF INCLUSIVE education are twofold: for students with disabilities to be full members of their schools and classroom groups, and for these students to make appropriate progress toward achieving academic and functional competence. Achieving these ambitious goals is most feasible when classmates with and without disabilities engage in shared learning activities and know how to relate and interact successfully with one another. Inclusive programming requires consideration of a number of cultural and structural elements that bear on the creation of a school program that is effective for diverse learners. These elements include an inclusive culture in the school, collaborative teaming among general and special educators, facilitation of positive relationships among students with disabilities and their typical peers, and the use of a range of curricular and instructional adaptations.

The primary focus of this article is on the instructional element: how teachers adapt instruction so that students with disabilities can learn in the context of general education classrooms with typical classmates. Studies of the perspectives of classroom teachers and students without disabilities on inclusion have shown that participation in classroom routines and instructional activities is crucial to a student's being perceived as a full member of a classroom group. Schnorr (1990) found that first graders perceived a part-time mainstreamed student with mental retardation as a visitor rather than as a class member, because the student did not share the same class assignments, activities, and peer networks. Likewise Peck, Gallucci, Staub, and Schwartz (1998) reported that "the children we interviewed consistently expressed the view that mere physical presence did not mean a child was a real member of the class. What was critical was participation" (p. 8).

Others who have studied inclusive classrooms have found that classroom teachers and the special education teachers with whom they collaborate begin their work together with only broad ideas about how they will partition their responsibilities and what sorts of adaptations students will need (Ferguson, Meyer, Jeanchild, Juniper, & Zingo, 1992; Giangreco, Dennis, Cloninger, Edelman, & Schattman, 1993; Janney & Snell, 1997). Classroom teachers learn to adapt instruction incidentally, by observing special education teachers working with the focus student. Janney and Snell (1997), in an investigation of the ways collaborating general and special education teachers sought to include students with disabilities in elementary classrooms, found that the many modifications made to teachers' roles, classroom routines, and instructional activities were part of an unstated agreement between the two teachers, but there was no explicit, written plan for the ways instructional practices would and would not be adapted.

In contrast to an incidental approach to making adaptations, this article describes a model for planning, using, and evaluating individualized adaptations. The model, which is adapted from Janney and Snell (2004), provides a set of decision rules and procedures for individualizing instruction for the range of exceptional students encountered in inclusive schools. Articulating the steps of the process and the criteria for choosing one possible adaptation over another gives educational teams a common language, thus assisting them to reach shared understandings of their joint work and the tasks required of each team member. Although the model and planning practices described here have not been formally field tested, they were originally generated by practicing master teachers in schools where virtually no one questions the membership of all students with disabilities. Further, these strategies are consistent with those promoted by many experts in inclusive education (Fisher, Sax, & Pumpian, 1999; Giangreco, Cloninger, & Iverson, 1998).

A Model for Making Individualized Adaptations

Despite the similarities in general and special education methods, some students with cognitive, neurological, physical, or social–behavioral disabilities require individualized adaptations to enable them to learn skills and knowledge appropriate to their age and abilities. The term *individualized adaptations* comprises the accommodations and modifications that are part of a student's individualized education plan (IEP). Thus, adaptations may include modified curriculum goals, changes made to learning-task requirements, specialized teaching methods and materials, altered testing procedures or conditions, assistive technology, and alterations to the physical environment. Special education students' accommodations and modifications are stated in general terms on their IEPs but must be applied on a day-to-day basis to specific lessons and activities. These more particular, applied adaptations are created through a collaborative problem-solving and planning process that occurs at varying intervals for various students (Snell & Janney, 2005).

Consistent with the dual social and academic goals of inclusive education, we apply two criteria for judging the appropriateness of adaptations: (a) they facilitate social and instructional participation in class activities, and (b) they do so using means that are *only as special as necessary*. Students' goals may be somewhat or extremely different from state and local curricular standards, but the adaptations provided should result in instructional participation. For instance, rather than merely being kept busy by coloring the worksheet used during a lesson on electric circuits, a student who does not write but can read some words could be provided printed labels to place in appropriate places on the worksheet, thus focusing participation on lesson content.

In addition to being instructionally appropriate, the most effective adaptations foster as much independence as possible and are suitable for the student's age and culture. An only-as-special-as-necessary approach to adaptations advises altering class routines and instructional activities only enough to enable the focus student to participate actively in achieving IEP goals. Receiving special education need not prevent students from engaging in ordinary activities and relationships.

Adaptations That Enhance Social and Instructional Outcomes

Making individualized adaptations that achieve the desired social and instructional goals is facilitated by understanding the variety of ways in which curriculum and methods can be adapted. The particularities of a given classroom and the individual needs and characteristics of the focus student may alter the sequence, but we propose using the following hierarchy of least-to-most-special adaptations as a general decision rule:

1. Consider the student's individualized learning goals and IEP accommodations.
2. Individualize the teaching methods.
3. Individualize the personal support.

Individualized Learning Goals

In an inclusive school, the scope of the curriculum is broadened to include a greater range of possible learning results. The existing general education core curriculum of basic skills and content areas must be expanded to accommodate multiple levels of skills and knowledge and additional goal areas (e.g., functional skills for use in daily life). The Individuals With Disabilities Education Improvement Act of 2004 requires that each IEP specify how the student's disability affects participation in the general curriculum, and the accommodations and modifications that are required for the student to access curriculum content and demonstrate learning.

The traditional curriculum can be adapted in three ways to meet students' individual needs: by supplementing, simplifying, or altering the curriculum goals. We intentionally refer to a student's curriculum *goals* being adapted in a particular goal area and do not suggest that a student be placed into a particular curriculum designation or track. However, at a particular point in time, a student's IEP goals may primarily reflect one of those three orientations.

Supplementary curriculum goals and accommodations. Many students' IEPs consist largely of accommodations, along with learning goals that supplement the general curriculum standards. These students include approximately 75% of those who qualify for special education, and are most often classified as having specific learning disabilities, speech–language impairments, or other health impairments (U.S. Department of Education, 2002). Supplementary goals may focus on remediation of basic skill deficits or on developing compensatory skills such as social, self-control, study, or organizational skills. For example, a middle school student who has a learning disability in reading and written language might be enrolled in a typical schedule of courses and participate fully in a regular academic curriculum. However, the student might have supplementary curriculum goals to improve reading, writing processes, and study skills. Such a student might also require accommodations such as preferential seating, extra time and oral testing for written tests, a laptop computer for taking notes, and word banks for class activities and tests. For a given lesson, this student might simply need the accommodation of a word bank or perhaps fewer items per page on a worksheet.

Simplified curriculum goals. Other students with IEPs—often those with cognitive disabilities who have basic literacy skills and can function almost independently given intermittent support—participate in the traditional subject areas but with simplified goals. That is, their goals are drawn from a lower grade level, are reduced in number, or require less complex types of learning (e.g., a student might memorize facts or apply a concept, whereas classmates have goals requiring analysis or evaluation).

A high school student with simplified curriculum goals might be enrolled in general-level academic core courses, a study hall or resource class, and electives that address vocational preparation. With content reduced and simplified to focus on carefully chosen basic concepts and useful skills, along with testing accommodations and adapted reading and writing demands, this student can maintain an academic presence in his or her school and also become prepared for life after school. Many states now have alternate grade level assessments and modified diplomas that can be attained by students who require simplified curricular goals.

Alternate curriculum goals. Students with more complex or severe disabilities (e.g., students with mental retardation requiring extensive supports or multiple physical and cognitive disabilities, who comprise less than 5% of the special education population) may have IEP goals that blend significantly simplified academics with alternate learning goals that emphasize the skills needed for immediate participation in daily life at school, at home, and in the community. In addition to learning self-help, recreational, and vocational activities, students learn to participate in school routines such as navigating the hallways and using the library and cafeteria. Also included are the functional academic skills (e.g., reading, writing, money, time management) and the motor, social, and communication skills needed to participate in daily activities. Despite their complex needs, when provided with suitable adaptations, students with severe disabilities can participate at least partially in most of the typical routines and activities of a regular class.

An elementary school student with, for example, a physical disability such as cerebral palsy as well as mental retardation, may have alternative curriculum goals that address communication, participation in self-help routines and class activities, and some very basic reading and arithmetic skills. Sample IEP goals might include (a) use augmentative devices and picture symbols to make choices and to relate recent events; (b) increase independence in school arrival/departure, classroom jobs, and lunch routines; (c) identify numerals and count objects to 20 in mathematics activities and functional contexts; (d) identify name in print; (e) make individualized contributions to cooperative group activities, given individualized adaptations to methods, materials, and personal assistance.

Although alternate curricular goals emphasize functionality, there are many general facts and knowledge, social skills, and recreational activities that may be included on a student's IEP because they are important to the student and the family and facilitate peer group membership and leading a normalized life.

Teaching students with a range of curricular goals. The use of this terminology—supplementary, simplified, and alternative—to describe curricular adaptations can help team members to communicate about the nature of students' IEP goals. The expanded, inclusive curriculum ensures that students are gaining as much access as possible to the general curriculum and age-appropriate activities. All students' IEP goals and lesson objectives, including those that are simplified or alternative, should be drawn directly from, or aligned with, the general curriculum. In a given lesson, all students' objectives can stem from or be aligned with a common learning standard. For example, in a unit on the life cycles of plants and animals, all students in a fifth-grade class might have the following goal: to describe and compare life cycles of plants and animals. Within a lesson on the stages of the life cycle of plants, instructional goals might be differentiated as follows:

- Regular lesson objective: Use scientific terms to describe the stages in the life cycle of a flowering plant.
- Accommodated lesson objective: Given a word bank of scientific terms, to arrange the stages of

the life cycle of a flowering plant in order and describe them.
- Simplified lesson objective: Given a word bank of selected scientific terms, to arrange the stages of the life cycle of a flowering plant in order and write brief (2–3 word) descriptions.
- Alternative/functional lesson objective: Given a word bank and pictures of the stages of the life cycle of a flowering plant, to match words with pictures and place them in order.

Individualized Teaching Methods

When efforts to individualize learning goals have not proven to be adequate, individualizing teaching methods and materials is the next step in the hierarchy. Instructional adaptations include any change in the instructional arrangement (e.g., teacher-directed whole class, teacher-directed small group, one-to-one, student-directed small group), the way students access content (e.g., listening to an oral presentation, reading and taking notes from a textbook, watching a demonstration, viewing a DVD), the teaching methods or strategies (e.g., direct instruction, inductive problem solving), and the way students practice or demonstrate learning (e.g., writing a report, building a model, completing a lab assignment, drawing a visual representation, answering questions orally, writing an essay). Adaptations can be made to any one or several of these elements of instruction.

In the hierarchy of least to most special adaptations, changing what the teacher does or provides—that is, the input—often is less intrusive than adapting what the student does. Examples of these sorts of instructional adaptations include (a) accompanying oral information with visuals: graphic organizers, maps, outlines; (b) providing models and demonstrations; (c) providing study guides of key concepts and vocabulary terms; and (d) reading test directions aloud. Teachers often find that although adaptations such as these may originally be made for a few students with IEPs, at times it is sensible to make them available for the entire classroom group. For example, if the special education teacher provides one or two students with learning disabilities with an adapted version of a written test that is constructed by listing multiple-choice items vertically rather than horizontally, providing additional white space between items, and judiciously reducing the test's readability level (unless reading is being tested), the classroom teacher may decide simply to adopt that test format for all students in the class.

In addition to adaptations to the instructional input, some students will also require adaptations to the output, or the tasks required of them. Among the many possible adaptations to the tasks or responses required of students are (a) completing only the specified problems on a math worksheet (e.g., the two-digit multiplication problems on a page of two- and three-digit problems), (b) taking lecture notes using a slot note format, (c) following picture cues to perform a multistep task, (d) giving oral rather than written responses to reading comprehension questions, and (e) completing a chart, map, or outline instead of writing an essay. In some cases students with complex learning needs may need alternative activities that relate to a class theme or project that they can do after having completed part of the general class activity. These activities might also be available to other students as supplementary or "cushion" tasks to do when assigned work has been completed.

Individualized Personal Support

The final stage, provision of personal support, is an adaptation that may be necessary for some students. Indeed, adding the help of a teacher or paraprofessional is often the first adaptation that comes to mind when considering the inclusion of students with severe disabilities. However, the addition of personal support also should follow the only-as-special-as-necessary guidelines. The use of peer rather than adult support should be considered, given that peers have been taught how to provide assistance (see Bond & Castagnera, this issue). Peer support is especially effective when peer-to-peer helping and peer-mediated instruction are typical practices and not reserved only for classmates with disabilities.

Clearly, there are situations in which adults need to provide physical assistance for a student (e.g., when being moved into or out of a wheelchair). But when adults provide personal support during instruction, it should be only during the activities or steps of activities for which it is essential; the aim should be to establish the student's participation in the activity, and then fade the assistance as soon as possible. As teachers experienced with inclusion advise, set it up and then back off.

Efficient Planning of Adaptations

How can teachers create these individualized adaptations in efficient yet systematic ways? Some teachers get quite good at winging it, but winging it can be stressful, inefficient, and not result in the most effective instruction. One helpful planning strategy is to approach the process in two phases. The first phase is to create *general adaptations*, which are patterns or formats for adapting the conventional routines and instructional designs used in the classroom. General adaptations are the customary ways that goals, methods, materials, and personal support are adapted for a student. It is possible to plan these general adaptations for repeated use over a semester or marking period because classrooms operate according to fairly predictable patterns and use a finite set of instructional practices. Planning for general adaptations requires knowledge of classroom routines, instructional formats, and the focus student's goals and support needs. However, once designed and communicated to the team, many general adaptations can be implemented with minimal day-to-day planning.

Then, *specific adaptations*, which apply to particular lessons, activities, or units, are developed. Specific adaptations must match the content or skills of a given lesson as well as the materials that are used. Whereas general adaptations can be planned once a semester, specific adaptations require some degree of short-term planning between the classroom teacher and special education staff.

For example, in high school social science classes, students typically take notes during lectures. A student who cannot keep up with these note-taking demands might be provided with slot notes, which are an outline of the lecture with words and phrases omitted so that the student is required to pay attention and fill in these blanks during the lecture. If the student has simplified curricular goals, the amount of material included in the slot notes also might be reduced. Providing the student with slot notes is a general adaptation: This adaptive strategy is used regularly whenever students are required to take notes. However, the content of the slot notes requires specific adaptations. The classroom teacher and the special educator, who has agreed to prepare the slot notes, must share information about the week's lecture content. Although the preparation of specific adaptations requires planning time, adaptations such as this can be filed in a course notebook so that they can be used again in the future if another student requires similar adaptations.

Planning Adaptations for Individual Students

The application of this adaptations model entails a series of steps. What follows is an abbreviated version of the steps detailed in Janney and Snell (2004). The steps vary according to students' ages, the complexity of their disabilities, and contextual variables such as whether the general and special education teachers are experienced collaborators. The amount of detail needed on the planning tools varies widely, and generally correlates with the extent to which the student's curricular goals differ from classmates' goals. Because it is not possible to describe or illustrate all of these variations here, we will use the example of a high school student whose IEP includes simplified curricular goals and supplementary goals in the area of self-management, as well as accommodations for test-taking and homework. We provide general descriptions of some of the tools that can be used to plan and communicate a student's individualized adaptations. In addition to the versions of these tools that appear in Janney and Snell (2004), similar tools may be found in Giangreco et al. (1998), and Fisher et al. (1999).

Gather and Share Information About the Students and the Classroom

The first step in creating individualized adaptations involves gathering and sharing information that will assist the classroom teacher to know the student and the special education teacher to know the classroom. Sharing this information enables the two teachers, along with other relevant team members, to create adaptations that fit both the student's needs and the classroom's academic demands and social expectations.

Information about the student. Essential to efficient and effective collaborative teaming is that all team members who will be in contact with a student have information about his or her intellectual, behavioral, physical, and social characteristics. Schools experienced with inclusion typically have an agreed-on school-wide approach for sharing this information. One helpful approach is to provide each relevant teacher and staff member with a two-sided form with the student's *program at-a-glance* on one side and a *student profile* on the other. The program-at-a-glance provides a concise summary of the student's IEP goals, accommodations, and any physical management or social-communication supports required by the IEP. The student information form might supply a brief description of the student's likes and dislikes, instructional or behavioral management strategies that do or do not work, and important information about the student's disability, communication abilities, assistive technology or adaptive equipment, and peer support approaches that have been used with the student. The student's IEP manager or special education service coordinator typically takes responsibility for completing these forms and for providing a copy to the classroom teacher and other relevant team members (e.g., instructional assistants and specialty teachers). The information provided by these tools will assist all educators who work with a student to make the needed accommodations and modifications.

Information about the classroom. Being a member of a class requires participation in classroom routines, instructional activities, and social relations, as well as following group norms and behavioral expectations. For an educational team to devise ways to include a student, all team members must have an understanding of the classroom's structure, curriculum, methods, and materials. An *assessment of classroom activities and procedures* comprises an inventory of the instructional formats and teaching methods used in the classroom as well as routines, rules, and other expectations. The most helpful way to obtain accurate information about the classroom is through a combination of teacher discussion and direct observation. The following are some of the aspects of the classroom's operating procedures with which any specialists who support students should be familiar: (a) the typical small group, large group, and independent instructional activities, and the frequently used student tasks/responses; (b) homework requirements; (c) textbooks and other frequently used materials; (d) test/quiz formats, frequency, and procedures; and (e) classroom rules and behavior management system, as well as norms for talking, moving around the classroom, leaving the room, etc.

Determine Which Adaptations Are Needed, and When

After this information is gathered, the next step in the process is to identify the tasks and activities that will require adaptations. Observing the focus student as he or she participates in classroom activities and routines yields information about the glitches in the student's participation. Teachers find that the time invested in completing such observations (which need to be conducted only once or twice per year) is far outweighed by the benefits accrued.

For the majority of students with IEPs, putting their accommodations into place will be the primary adaptations required. For students with simplified or alternative curriculum goals, the special education and general education teachers should collaboratively decide which of the classroom activities, routines, and materials will need general and/or specific adaptations, and what the procedure will be for designing, delivering, and monitoring those adaptations.

A student with simplified or reduced curriculum goals and a moderate level of support needs will seldom require adaptations to participate in most classroom activities. For instance, a student in a high school core course might need (a) slot notes for lectures, (b) partner reading when silent reading assignments are made, (c) pairing with particular classmates for cooperative groups or peer tutoring, (d) study guides for tests, with the sources of information noted, (e) oral reading of tests, and (f) reduced homework assignments. Of these adaptations, the only ones that would require specific adaptations made on a regular basis are the slot notes, study guides, tests, and homework assignments. These specific adaptations would be based on the content (reducing the number of concepts and terms) and any instructional adaptations that must match a particular assignment. The general adaptations would simply be in place for as long as they were appropriate for the student. Decisions about a student's ongoing adaptations should be recorded and communicated with all adults who work with the student. An *individualized adaptations plan* that lists these general adaptations and indicates the specific adaptations that should be planned weekly or biweekly can typically be recorded on one or two pages, and needs to be revised only if problems arise.

For students who have some alternate curricular goals, an additional step is required: The team must determine when to address these goals during the daily schedule. The *program planning matrix* is a planning tool that aids this process. To construct the matrix, the student's IEP goals are listed in the left-hand column of a table, and the class activity schedule appears in the top row, creating a table with cells corresponding to each possible goal–activity combination. Decisions are then made about when the student's alternate goals will be taught. Although most simplified academic goals can be addressed at the same time as classmates study those same subject areas, the student should receive instruction in his or her functional life skills during naturally occurring times across the day.

Implement and Evaluate Adaptations

The evaluation of individualized adaptations refers back to their purposes—student achievement and class membership. Achievement, of course, is measured by progress on IEP goals. Class membership is a less tangible metric, but can be assessed informally through the use of strategies such as time sampling to estimate the amount of time that the focus student is engaged in academic instruction and/or social interactions with peers, or more formally using sociometric techniques (Janney & Snell, 2006). Another potentially helpful evaluation measure is to keep records of whether adaptations were in fact implemented as planned.

The general education and special education collaborative team that serves a student or students also can benefit from evaluating the effectiveness of their team processes and the fulfillment of their individual roles and responsibilities. For instance, classroom teachers should regularly be asked questions about the clarity of their role in the student's educational programming and the appropriateness of adaptations and any in-class support provided by specialists (Janney & Snell, 2004). As for the other steps in this process, we recommend explicit problem solving among team members regarding how, when, and by whom these tasks will be accomplished.

Conclusion

The approach to individualized adaptations presented here is intended to help teachers in inclusive classrooms to make adaptations to schoolwork that are both effective and created by a process that is feasible in the context of the busy life of schools. The model and the planning tools here evolve as they are used and adapted by teams of teachers in the numerous schools across the country that are seeking to create learning communities that serve all students. We strongly recommend adopting uniform planning and communication forms for a school, grade level, or department. This uniformity helps to establish the expectation that systematic planning and evaluation of adaptations will occur; it also facilitates students' transition from one grade level to the next. Using a logical planning process and agreed-on criteria for selecting adaptations promotes greater belonging and achievement for students and makes the process less time consuming for teachers.

When individualized adaptations are required, the ideal planning process occurs through collaboration by the special education and general education teachers at the outset of each unit of instruction. Collaborative planning helps to ensure that adaptations fit with the general instructional plan. Such planning considers all students' goals, common activities and projects, and the supplementary or alternative activities that can serve the interests of students with and without IEPs.

Even if they consider the amount of adult effort and involvement required to meet the learning needs of all students within common classes to be reasonable, some readers are likely to feel slightly (or even acutely) daunted by the task that lies before them. This can be especially true if a school has not established the school-wide structural and cultural conditions that foster inclusion. One tactic for maintaining motivation and energy to move forward is to seek the affective and instrumental support of colleagues and parents who share an interest in the goals of inclusive programming. Apprehension also will abate if readers bear these points in mind: (a) strategies that prepare the school environment by nurturing the inclusive values, attitudes, and perceptions foster the development of a culture that significantly eases the way for the use of accommodating teaching practices as well as individualized adaptations; (b) the vast majority of students with disabilities do not require day-to-day individualized planning of adaptations once general adaptations have been agreed-on; and (c) only a very small proportion of students require individualized support plans and ongoing, weekly or monthly team planning. This is not to say that instituting inclusive practices is not challenging. Learning any new skill or process can make one feel inept or frustrated.

However, teachers who have implemented the practices described in this article repeatedly report satisfaction with the results and are willing to continue their efforts because of the beneficial outcomes for themselves and their students.

References

Ferguson, D. L., Meyer, G., Jeanchild, J., Juniper, L., & Zingo, J. (1992). Figuring out what to do with the grownups: How teachers make inclusion "work" for students with disabilities. *Journal of the Association for Persons With Severe Handicaps, 17,* 218–226.

Fisher, D., Sax, C., & Pumpian, I. (1999). *Inclusive high schools: Learning from the contemporary classroom.* Baltimore: Brookes.

Giangreco, M. F., Cloninger, C. J., & Iverson, V. S. (1998). *Choosing outcomes and accommodations for children (COACH).* Baltimore: Brookes.

Giangreco, M. F., Dennis, R., Cloninger, C., Edelman, S., & Schattman, R. (1993). "I've counted Jon": Transformational experiences of teachers educating students with disabilities. *Exceptional Children, 59,* 359–372.

Individuals With Disabilities Education Improvement Act of 2004, Pub. L. No. 108-446, 118 Stat. 2647 (2004).

Janney, R., & Snell, M. E. (1997). How teachers include students with moderate and severe disabilities in elementary classes: The means and meaning of inclusion. *Journal of the Association for Persons With Severe Handicaps, 22,* 159–169.

Janney, R., & Snell, M. E. (2004). *Teachers' guides to inclusive practices: Modifying schoolwork.* (2nd ed.). Baltimore: Brookes.

Janney, R., & Snell, M. E. (2006). *Teachers' guides to inclusive practices: Social relationships and peer support* (2nd ed). Baltimore: Brookes.

Peck, C. A., Gallucci, C., Staub, D., & Schwartz, I. (1998, April). *The function of vulnerability in the creation of inclusive classroom communities: Risk and opportunity.* Paper presented at the annual meeting of The American Educational Research Association, San Diego, CA.

Schnorr, R. F. (1990). "Peter? He comes and goes … ": First graders' perspectives on a part-time mainstream student. *Journal of the Association for Persons With Severe Handicaps, 15,* 231–240.

Snell, M. E., & Janney, R. (2005). *Teachers' guides to inclusive practices: Collaborative teaming* (2nd ed.). Baltimore: Brookes.

U.S. Department of Education. (2002). *Twenty-fourth annual report to Congress on the implementation of the Individuals With Disabilities Education Act.* Jessup, MD: Author.

Rebecca Bond
Elizabeth Castagnera

Peer Supports and Inclusive Education: An Underutilized Resource

Successful inclusion of students with disabilities in general education classrooms requires a variety of supports. This article demonstrates the role that peers can play in supporting each other. Whole-classroom strategies such as Class-Wide Peer Tutoring (CWPT) and cross-age tutoring are highlighted as methods of supporting inclusive education. Information is also provided about peer tutoring efforts at the secondary level in which students receive elective credit for supporting students with disabilities in general education classes. Suggestions for providing guidance and support for peer tutors are included. Further, this article explores the concept of establishing a cooperative classroom by addressing the 4 types of helping that must become common to all classrooms: requesting help, accepting help, refusing help, and providing help.

Rebecca Bond is a teacher at Valhalla High School. Elizabeth Castagnera is a teacher at Santana High School.

Correspondence should be addressed to Rebecca Bond, E-mail: rbond27@znet.com or Elizabeth Castagnera, E-mail: llcast@cox.net.

IN THESE DAYS of diminishing resources, pressure to meet standards, and an increase in diverse ability levels in classrooms, educators must find cost-effective ways to support all students. A variety of supports and services must be in place for inclusive schooling to become a reality for students. One of our most readily available supports for students is other students. Although it may be necessary at times to use paraprofessionals to support inclusive education, there are many instances when it is more beneficial to use peers. Miller and Miller (as cited in The Access Center, n.d.) found that using peers to support students with disabilities is an effective intervention, educationally and economically, and it benefits the tutor and tutee, socially and educationally, by motivating them to learn.

In this article, we describe practices and strategies for using peers to support inclusive education. We also describe how a peer tutor course at the secondary level can be used to effectively support students with disabilities in general education classes. Finally, we discuss the concept of creating a cooperative classroom to support all students.

Class-Wide Peer Tutoring (CWPT)

CWPT was first developed in the late 1970s as an intervention for improving student learning in urban classrooms. Initial research indicated that it was successful in increasing academic skills for all students participating. However, recent research has proven that it also builds social interaction skills between students with and without disabilities (Snell & Janney, 2000).

With the CWPT approach, a student with higher academic ability is paired with a student with lower academic ability. Materials are developed so that they are individualized to each student in the pair, and each student is trained on how to instruct the other. With this approach, the tutor–tutee role is rotated so that each person in the pair has an opportunity to be the tutor. The rotation of roles is important because it gives each student in the pair the opportunity to benefit from teaching the other student. When children teach children, there is improvement in student learning (Greenwood, Carta, & Kamps, 1990). Students become *prosumers,* meaning they are producers and consumers of education (National Self-Help Clearinghouse, 2002).

Peer-Assisted Learning Strategies (PALS)

A version of CWPT that is very well established is PALS. The PALS approach to reading involves students being paired up for 40-min sessions, three times a week. As with the CWPT approach described previously, both students in the pair are given the opportunity to be in the tutor role in each session. The interactions between tutors and tutees are highly structured, so that the person in the tutor role has a script to follow to correct and reward the tutee. Teachers have found this structure to allow for less interpretation on the tutor's part, which many tutors appreciate. For example, in a high school English class, Katie used the following PALS script when tutoring Sarah, a student with lower reading skills. Katie read the material first and then Sarah reread the same text. Whenever a word-reading error occurred, Katie said, "Stop. You missed that word. Can you figure it out?" Sarah either figured the word out on her own within 4 sec, or Katie said, "That word is _____. What word?" Sarah then said the word, and Katie said, "Good. Read the sentence again."

Documentation exists to show that PALS is an effective method for improving reading fluency and comprehension for students with learning disabilities as well as for those who may be considered low- or average-achieving students. Due to the positive results, PALS is considered a best practice by the U.S. Department of Education Program Effectiveness Panel for Inclusion (Fuchs et al., 2001).

Cross-Age Tutoring Programs

Cross-age tutoring has been proven to be very successful, especially in the area of literacy. It has been shown that the tutor and the tutee make substantial gains in vocabulary, reading accuracy, self-correction, and comprehension (Marious, 2000). Cross-age tutoring generally involves an older student taking on the role of tutor and the younger student taking on the role of tutee. An older student who is performing at grade level may tutor a younger student who is just learning the material being taught. Although older students may be covering material that they have previously mastered, they are more likely to remember the material if they are putting that knowledge to some purpose (Topping, 1988). Another possibility is that an older student with a disability could tutor a younger student. While the younger student is learning new skills, the older student is learning tutoring skills and reinforcing specific content skills. Cross-age tutoring supports inclusive education in that it may eliminate the need for pull-out by the resource specialist. Teachers sometimes structure their classes so that all students participate in tutoring at some level, taking advantage of the benefits of tutoring. At the high school level, this may involve special projects in the community. For example, Maggie, a student with a developmental disability who was reading at a first-grade level, participated in a senior project with her high school where she spent time reading to younger students at a local elementary school on a weekly basis. She was able to read books that challenged her reading level in a setting that was meaningful and reinforcing to her. Maggie experienced significant gains in her ability to decode written material as well as an increase in her self-esteem.

Numerous studies exist that demonstrate the effectiveness of cross-age tutoring. For example, Fisher (2001) conducted a study comparing two middle schools on the effectiveness of cross-age tutoring. Struggling readers were identified at both schools. Students at one school tutored first- and second-graders in reading, whereas students in the control school attended a remedial reading class. In tests conducted at the end of the school year, students who participated in the tutoring (the tutor and the tutee) outperformed the students who did not participate in tutoring in the vocabulary subsection and the comprehension subsection of the Gates-MacGintie Reading Tests. In addition, the students who tutored also outperformed the students who did not tutor in the statewide achievement test (Fisher, 2001).

Providing the opportunity for students with disabilities to tutor other students is a key feature of tutoring programs. Students with disabilities are typically put in a position where they are the ones receiving help or being tutored, leading to perceptions of academic inadequacy. As in Maggie's case, self-esteem increases when students have the opportunity to successfully teach someone else. The feeling of being useful is especially important for high school students who are at risk (Duckenfield, 1995).

Peer Tutoring at a Secondary Level

Once students enter middle and high school, the structure of their school day changes dramatically compared to their elementary years. When students with disabilities are included in general education classes, they attend a variety of classes with many different teachers for the first time. It can be challenging for special education teachers to provide support and meet students' needs when all of their students are in different classes every period. A *peer tutor elective course* is a creative and useful way of meeting the needs of students with disabilities who are in general education classes.

Through the elective course, the peer tutor attends the general education class with the student with a disability, providing one-on-one support as needed. Rather than being enrolled in the general education class, the peer tutor is enrolled in a peer tutor elective class taught by the special education teacher. It has been found that the student with the disability and the peer tutor benefit academically. Students who receive instruction from their peers make academic gains (Villa & Thousand, 1996) and peer tutors have demonstrated academic growth in the areas in which they are tutoring (Bond, 2001). Students with disabilities have increased their grades in general education classes with the addition of peer tutor support. In return, peer tutors have made comments such as, "I have learned more about biology as a peer tutor than I did when I took the class myself last year!" and "Being a peer tutor in a math class has definitely made me do better in my own math class."

Some peer tutors may provide support for only part of the class. One student, Allen, attended a 3-D art class and needed peer tutor support to only understand the directions that were given at the beginning of each class. The peer tutor attended class with Allen for the first 15 min, clarifying the directions and demonstrating the assignment as needed. For the rest of the period Allen relied on the general educator and *natural supports* (other students in the class) for any additional assistance he needed. The peer tutor then went to a science class to assist Joel, who needed support only during labs that took place during the second half of class.

Some students may need a peer tutor only for certain classes and attend other classes independently. Stephanie requires a peer tutor for support in her English, history, and science classes. However, she attends her aerobics, art, and computer classes independently. Some students have individual education plan (IEP) goals that focus on fading peer tutor support to promote greater independence, whereas others have IEP goals to fade paraprofessional support by adding peer tutor support.

Peer tutors can provide support in various ways, including help in locating classes, taking notes, reading materials aloud, and providing basic curricular modifications. Often students with disabilities need directions and assignments clarified; therefore, peer tutors' responsibilities include ensuring that their tutees understand what is expected of them. Peer tutors are available to keep the students engaged and answer questions as needed. The importance of providing support versus doing the work for a student is strongly emphasized. In addition, it is important to note that the idea is not to create a separate island within the classroom for the student with a disability and the peer tutor. Therefore, part of the responsibility of a peer tutor is to facilitate the inclusion of the student with a disability in class discussions and activities to the maximum extent possible. Peer tutors are an invaluable resource, as they are able to provide the individualized support necessary for students with disabilities to succeed within the general education classroom.

The Peer Tutor Course

Bond and Castagnera (2003) describe an effective model for a peer tutor course. In this model, peer tutors are initially matched with another student based on grade level, courses in which they have been previously or are currently enrolled, and subject interests. Peer tutors check in with the special education teacher at the beginning of class to receive curricular modifications (if required) and instruction on how to meet that student's needs for the day's activities. The peer tutors are given a daily journal in which they are to record activities that take place in class, the student's participation, and any homework assignments. They also indicate any areas of need the student may have, as well as any support they need as peer tutors. The peer tutor then attends the general education class with the student. While in the class, the peer tutor takes direction from the general education teacher. Approximately 5 min before the class is over, the peer tutor returns to the special education teacher and shares what occurred in class and any specific communication from the general education teacher.

According to Snell and Janney (2000), "Peer tutors need to receive training to be effective" (p. 136). Peer tutors are provided with five training sessions. On training days, general education teachers receive notice that peer tutors will not be in class and are asked to use natural supports to provide assistance to the student with a disability. The benefits of the training outweighs the absence of peer tutors on these days.

The five training sessions are led by the special education teacher and are given over a period of a few weeks. Each session has a corresponding homework assignment that relates to the topic discussed. The first session provides opportunities for an in-depth discussion of inclusive education and includes the topics of equity, fairness, and special education laws. It exposes the students to People First Language (e.g., saying "people with disabilities" instead of "the disabled") and the impact language has on the acceptance of diversity. The second session teaches peer tutors a variety of simple teaching strategies and ways to provide simple on-the-spot modifications and accommodations to meet tutees' needs. The third session enables tutors to gain a better understanding of specific learning disabilities. They also learn how behavior relates to communication, especially for students who have difficulty communicating or who do not communicate verbally. In the fourth session, peer tutors are encouraged to reflect on how important friendships are in their own lives so they can begin to see the importance of their role in facilitating friendships for their tutees.

During the final training session, peer tutors are asked to share what they, as well as the students with disabilities, have learned over the semester. This can be demonstrated through a portfolio consisting of a collection of works such as class assignments, tests, photographs, and reflections written by teachers or by students themselves. Peer tutors can present their portfolios using a variety of media, including PowerPoint presentations and videotapes. In addition to being a tool for the peer tutors to reflect on their own experiences, these portfolios can be presented by the students with disabilities at their IEP meetings. For example, Natalie, a peer tutor, worked closely with the speech and language pathologist while supporting

Tim in his English class. Tim gave weekly speeches in his class, each time working on improving articulation. Several of the students' speeches were recorded throughout the school year. Natalie's final project included recorded clips that showed the progress Tim had made in the area of articulation, as well as information about what Natalie learned in regard to supporting students with articulation difficulties.

Due to the importance of consistency, peer tutors are expected to attend class every day. They are graded on the quality of their support, their positive interaction skills, and on-the-job work habits, which include following directions, showing initiative, accepting responsibility, and communicating ideas, questions, and needs. Their grades are also based on completion of homework assignments from the training sessions, as well as their final projects. Special and general educators are responsible for evaluating peer tutors.

If it is determined by the educators that a peer tutor is not working successfully with a particular student or in a particular class, a change in assignment is considered for that peer tutor. If all possibilities are exhausted and no other match can be made, the peer tutor can assist the special education teacher in making modifications or other tasks rather than attending a class with a student.

A Cooperative Classroom

In the true sense of inclusive education, it needs to be clear that all students are welcomed, appreciated, and valued members of the classroom, no matter what their differences may be. A sense of community must become an integral component of a classroom if all students are to learn the value of each individual and achieve their highest potential. According to Snell and Janney (2000), "Cooperative learning classrooms are places where heterogeneous groups of students learn to work together and accept one another while also achieving positive academic and social outcomes" (p. 140).

Many students with disabilities may need help and support throughout their entire lives, as is true of any individual. One of the ways educators can create a cooperative environment is to establish classroom norms that are based on the assumption that all people need help, not just students with disabilities. It should become a classroom norm that giving and receiving help is positive and that everyone involved will benefit when they help each other. Sapon-Shevin (1999) offers four types of helping that must become common to all classrooms:

1. Asking for help appropriately—"Could you help me with this?"
2. Offering help respectfully—"Would it help if I read that problem out loud for you?"
3. Accepting help graciously—"Thanks for noticing I needed help with that."
4. Rejecting help kindly—"No thanks, I have my own way I'm trying to do this."

Optimally, in cooperative classrooms, students with disabilities are not the only ones to receive help, and they provide help as well. Students can be taught that although some students may appear to need more help than others, all students need help in certain situations. Teachers can make this clear by encouraging students to adopt the four types of helping described previously, and by deliberately asking others (adults and students) for help in front of their students. When teachers encourage students to help and be helped, students learn the value of working cooperatively, within the classroom as well as in their own communities.

Conclusion

Tutoring is successful for many reasons. Studies have shown that cross-age and same-age peer-mediated strategies are as effective or more effective than traditional teacher-mediated practices for students with and without disabilities across a variety of subject areas (Greenwood, Carta, & Kamps, 1990).

Researchers are learning that for inclusive education to be meaningful and effective, peer-to-peer relationships are more than an outcome; they are a critical component of the process of inclusive education (Kennedy, 2003). Inclusive education helps us work toward creating a society where all people are valued. When peers are used to support inclusive education, everyone benefits. Students with disabilities are afforded an appropriate education in the least restrictive environment, the general education class. Students without disabilities are given opportunities to increase their academic skills, gain a better understanding and acceptance of diversity, and improve their communication and social skills.

When teachers use support strategies in their classrooms such as CWPT, cross-age tutoring, peer tutoring, and cooperative learning, students see how people can work together. They develop an understanding that everyone belongs. They see a small-scale example of what society can and should be like. Once students leave the educational system, they shape their world based on the education they were provided in elementary and secondary school. Using peer supports truly makes a difference—for individual students and for society as a whole.

References

The Access Center: Improving Access for All Students K–8. (n.d.) *Using peer tutoring to facilitate access.* Retrieved February 2005, from http://www.k8accesscenter.org/training_resources/documents/PeerTutoringFinal.doc

Bond, R. J. (2001). *Peer tutors of students with moderate and severe disabilities in general education high school settings.* Unpublished master's project, San Diego State University, California.

Bond, R., & Castagnera, E. (2003). Supporting one another: Peer tutoring in an inclusive San Diego high school. In D. Fisher & N. Frey (Eds.), *Inclusive urban schools* (pp. 119–143). Baltimore: Brookes.

Duckenfield, M. (1995). *Performance of at risk students.* Clemson, SC: National Dropout Prevention Center.

Fisher, D. (2001). Cross-age tutoring: Alternatives to the reading resource room for struggling adolescent readers. *Journal of Instructional Psychology, 28,* 234–237.

Fuchs, D., Fuchs, L. S., Thompson, A., Svenson, E., Yen, L., Al Otaiba, S., et al. (2001). Peer-assisted learning strategies in reading: Extensions for kindergarten, first grade, and high school. *Remedial and Special Education, 22*(1), 15–21.

Greenwood, C. R., Carta, J. J., & Kamps, D. (1990). Teacher-mediated versus peer-mediated instruction: A review of educational advantages and disadvantages. In H. C. Foot, M. J. Morgan, & R. H. Shute (Eds.), *Children helping children* (pp. 177–205). New York: Wiley.

Kennedy, C. H. (2003). Peer-to-peer relationships as a foundation for inclusive education. In D. Fisher & N. Frey (Eds.), *Inclusive urban schools* (pp. 143–149). Baltimore: Brookes.

Marious, S. E. (2000). Mix and match: The effects of cross-age tutoring on literacy. *Reading Improvement, 37,* 126–128.

National Self-Help Clearinghouse, Peer Research Laboratory. (2002). *Peer tutoring works both ways.* Retrieved February 5, 2005, from http://selfhelpweb.org/peer.html

Sapon-Shevin, M. (1999). *Because we can change the world: A practical guide to building cooperative, inclusive classroom communities.* Needham Heights, MA: Allyn & Bacon.

Snell, M. E., & Janney, R. (2000). *Social relationships and peer support.* Baltimore: Brookes.

Topping, K. (1988). *The peer tutoring handbook.* Cambridge, MA: Brookline Books.

Villa, R. A., & Thousand, J. S. (1996). Student collaboration: An essential for curriculum delivery in the 21st century. In S. Stainback & W. Stainback (Eds.), *Inclusion: A guide for educators* (pp. 171–191). Baltimore: Brookes.

Nancy K. French
Ritu V. Chopra

Teachers as Executives

The roles and responsibilities of special educators have shifted as schools move to provide inclusive services for students with disabilities. The inclusive special educator is responsible for coordinating a complex system of adults and students—often including paraeducators, related service specialists, classroom teachers, and peer assistants. This contemporary role is analogous to that of an executive in business settings and requires comparable leadership, collaboration, and communication skills. Teachers who demonstrate skills in 5 key functioning areas may see more successful inclusion of their students. Of importance, teachers who are adjusting to the shift in role require certain administrative supports as they acquire this new identity of executive.

THE ANALOGY OF TEACHER as executive was first introduced by David Berliner over 20

Nancy K. French is Research Professor of Education at the University of Colorado at Denver and Health Sciences Center. Ritu V. Chopra is Director of the PAR²A Center at the University of Colorado at Denver and Health Sciences Center.

Correspondence should be sent to Nancy K. French, University of Colorado at Denver and Health Sciences Center, 1380 Lawrence Street, Suite 650, Denver, CO 80204. E-mail: nancy.french@cudenver.edu

years ago. Berliner (1983a, 1983b) compared teacher roles to those of midlevel executives in businesses. He likened the responsibilities of directing and managing the work of students and of classroom assistants and volunteers to that of directing, organizing, and monitoring workers' accomplishments. He compared the curriculum planning of teachers to the visioning of executives in businesses and lesson plans to the strategic planning necessary to achieve the mission.

Berliner, however, could not have foreseen how accurate his analogy would become in only 2 decades. In special education, a fast-growing knowledge base led to increased emphasis on community-based instruction (Falvey, 1986), neighborhood school placement (Brown et al., 1989), access for students with disabilities to core curriculum (e.g., Individuals With Disabilities Education Act, [IDEA] of 1990), and achievement of high academic standards for all students (Individuals With Disabilities Education Act Amendments of 1997; Individuals With Disabilities Education Improvement Act of 2004; No Child Left Behind Act of 2001). With the changes in programmatic emphasis for students with disabilities, the need for differentiated staffing patterns became apparent. More personnel were required to provide state-of-the-art services to students with disabilities, and hiring patterns rapidly shifted toward greater proportions of lesser-trained personnel, known as paraeducators or instructional assistants (French & Pickett, 1997). Evidence of this shift lies in the numbers. Although the student population in U.S. public schools increased by about 13% during the 1990s, the number of teachers increased by about 18%. At the same time, the employment of paraeducators increased at a national average of 48% (U.S. Department of Education, Institute of Education Sciences, National Center for Educational Statistics, 2005).

The Corresponding Shift in Teacher Role

Fisher, Frey, & Thousand (2003) aptly pointed out that "The environments, activities, and expectations for students with disabilities are changing" (p. 43). They called for a dramatic departure from the traditional categorical preparation of teachers because today's special educators perform different roles than their counterparts of the 1980s and, therefore, need different kinds of knowledge, skills, and dispositions. Their research revealed five essential roles of contemporary special educators in inclusive schools: instruction, assessment, communication, leadership, and record keeping (Fisher et al., 2003). Similarly, French (2003) has characterized the special education teacher in the role of an executive that includes five main areas of responsibility: planning, assessment, instruction, collaboration, and paraeducator supervision. However, the executive that French alludes to cannot be likened to the manager who performs routine or perfunctory administrative tasks. French's description of the teacher's role as an executive is more comparable to modern leadership theorists' notions of shared expertise and distributed or balanced leadership (McNulty & Bailey, 2004; Spillane, Halverson, & Diamond, 2001).

Data Sources

This article is based on three experiences and corresponding information sources. First, we have taught a course in paraeducator supervision over 60 times in 32 different states (French, 1999, 2000). The course content was originally based on teacher supervision concepts described by numerous researchers and theorists (e.g., Fullan, 1990; Garman, 1986; Garmston, 1987, 1988; Glatthorn, 1997). During the course, we employ a structured activity in which teachers describe their experiences in working with paraeducators. We have recorded their responses and found that the themes include problems and promising practices.

Second, in 1996–1997 we conducted a study about the paraeducator role in inclusion in which we conducted focus group interviews with four participant groups: parents of students with disabilities, special educators, general educators, and paraeducators (French & Chopra, 1999). Although the original focus of the study was on paraeducators, the findings also illuminated the role of teacher as the leader or program executive. Moreover, the findings emphasized the importance of collaborating with other adults, supervising paraeducators, planning for modifications, ensuring appropriate instruction and appropriate supports, and assessing student and programmatic outcomes.

Third, in 2002 we conducted a study of the relationships among the adults in inclusive programs. The interview data from special educators, paraeducators, general educators, and the parents of elementary students with significant support needs led to the conclusion that the teacher is the central figure and the determining factor in the success of inclusion (Chopra, 2002; Chopra & French, 2004).

In this article, we feature two stories that illustrate the differences in the roles that teachers play. In the first, the teacher saw herself as a leader and employed executive-like behaviors and the inclusion of students with significant needs was deemed a success by all accounts. In the second, the teacher had good intentions but was not able to hold meetings or establish other important communication supports among team members and the respondents believed that inclusion was not working very well.

Jamie's Story

Jamie, a veteran teacher of students requiring significant instructional support, has been at

Mount Evans Elementary for only a year. She believes in full inclusion. In her words,

> Successful inclusion is when children with special needs in a regular education classroom are getting the same opportunities as everybody else, where they have a learning outcome for every single part of their day. It may be the same learning outcome as the other kids. It may be a modified learning outcome. It may be a totally different learning outcome. But that is identified and that is being worked on.

Jamie refuses to pull students out of general education classrooms; she sees it as her role to integrate her services into the classroom. She plans curricular modifications and adaptations according to each student's individualized education program (IEP) so that students may fully participate in the classroom. She says, "What I try to really do is immerse myself into the classroom from the time they get here to the time they leave."

Teamwork is more than just a philosophy. She stresses this to paraeducators, teachers, and other service providers. Her motto is "We think as a team. We make decisions as a team and we all implement as a team." She insists

> Inclusion would not be possible without teamwork. It is not one person's job even if the person is doing their best. One teacher could not do all the accommodations that need to happen for that child. It would be so much work for that regular ed. teacher to have to do everything that would need to be done for that child.

Helga, a paraeducator who works with Jamie, concurs, "It's really, truly, a team that Jamie has created ... everything is a team effort. Everybody is included and even the principal is involved."

Jamie's actions demonstrate her belief that communication is vital to teamwork—ongoing communication builds trust for teamwork. Every week, Jamie's schedule includes formal, sit-down, or telephone meetings with school professionals, paraeducators, and parents.

During her meeting with the classroom teachers, she shares the curriculum modifications and adaptations she has planned for the students. She also spends time clarifying teachers' and paraeducators' roles in implementing the modified curriculum. According to Jamie, "I just want to make sure that they feel supported and they have guidance and kind of know where to go or what the next steps are." The meetings also provide a forum for addressing other issues or concerns about students or families.

She holds similar meetings with other service providers, including the occupational therapists, physical therapist, school nurse, and speech language pathologist. Jamie uses these meetings as platforms to make sure that everyone is on the same page.

In her meetings with paraeducators, Jamie conveys information from other meetings with teachers and parents to paraeducators. In these meetings the paraeducators give feedback about the effectiveness of what they implement in the classroom in terms of what works and what does not work in a particular situation with a child. When in the classroom, the paraeducators use data sheets on which they record how the child is progressing with reference to his or her IEP goals. Jamie values the feedback because it helps her to decide what needs to be changed or tightened or continued in the program for each child.

In addition to the weekly scheduled meeting before school, Jamie and the paraeducators touch base with each other during the day and at the end of each day to address any problems or issues that need immediate attention. Under Jamie's supervision paraeducators know the boundaries of their role. One mother says, "Jamie definitely sets the tone and they [paraeducators] know where the boundaries are. ... I like that because I feel like she's the boss and they know that. And so if there's a problem, they seem to go through her." According to the paraeducators and classroom teachers, Jamie is always accessible, available, and willing to talk.

As a weekly practice, Jamie has a regular half-hour scheduled appointment with one or both parents of each student on her caseload. These appointments are either face to face or by telephone, depending on the parent's wishes. During the meetings she apprises the parents of the child's all-around progress and addresses questions and concerns. She helps the parents connect activities and strategies at home with those followed at school. Jamie gives the following example: "We talk about what big academic units are coming, what is the child's learning going to look like for those activities, and what's homework going to look like so parents are linked in with the homework piece."

Jamie recognizes that time is a rare commodity, but everyone in the team realizes the importance and usefulness of the meetings. Everyone involved makes time for the weekly meeting because working and planning together makes each individual's job easier and more efficient. As Jamie explains:

> It's driven by all of us. But I think the key is that it has to be a priority. This is something we have to do. We have to meet. We have to talk. We have to communicate. Once you prioritize it as a team, people will make time to do it. ... You have to get flexible with your scheduling.

Everyone attributes the success of the program to Jamie's leadership and her executive-like demeanor. One parent put it this way: "She's just on top of everything. ... Jamie is very effective, and if you did not have as effective a leader in the team, then things would be different." Stacey, a classroom teacher agrees, "Jamie is an amazing leader. She is so involved. ... I've had other situations with kids with special education needs where it hasn't been very effective because of the special education teacher."

Judy, another parent, who works as a dietician, is convinced that under Jamie's leadership every member of the team has a clear understanding of their roles. Judy compares the existing team to a well run team in the medical field:

> In the medical field, you have the doctor and the physical therapist and the occupational therapist and the nurse and everybody's in sync. You talk about a patient and every discipline gives their input, and when you have a well run team like that there's nothing better. When every piece of the puzzle is doing what they're supposed to ... the patient is getting the best possible care. I feel like that's what we've got right here right now. Everybody's doing what they're supposed to do in their role.

Dan's Story

At Fox Trail Elementary, Dan, the special education teacher divides his time among nine students with significant support needs. As a second-year teacher, Dan realizes the importance of collaboration among school professionals to make it possible for all children to participate to the best of their abilities. In his words:

> Successful inclusion would be having the student included in the culture of the school, to the maximum what they're capable of, having them in their classroom as much as possible, participating in social and academic activities. ... Having the teacher, the paraeducator, and myself in a joint collaboration, so that all three of those people are involved in planning and implementing the goals for the student.

Dan also believes that for inclusion to be successful, it is important to recognize "parents as partners" and give them "a feeling that the school is on their side or is their partner and that we're not working against them." Dan stresses the importance of being "open to input and willing to hear the other person to come to a mutual agreement."

Philosophically, the parents, paraeducators, and classroom teachers who work with Dan all agree that successful inclusion is a result of a collaborative team effort and open communication. However, in practice, the program is riddled with miscommunication and it lacks leadership. Communications among team members are primarily informal. The only formal meeting is the annual IEP meeting.

One parent, Barbara, is frustrated with the lack of feedback and follow-through after decisions are made at IEP meetings. She elaborates, "It's almost like you have too many people involved. Everyone has their piece and some people don't do their piece." She laments, "I wish people were more proactive." She attributes the problem to miscommunication resulting from conflicting expectations of team members. Barbara stressed the need for one person to coordinate the work of the team so everyone does their part and everything gets done.

Dan's schedule includes no time during the day to meet with people. He explains, "I try to catch them when I can and let them know what I see for that day or if there's something going on." Clare, one of the paraeducators, confirms that Dan often seeks her input, not in scheduled meetings but in passing and casual interactions. Although Clare expresses no particular dissatisfaction with the impromptu guidance she receives, she is wistful about the need for team meetings, "In the ideal world it would be nice to have more time and more team meetings." On the other hand, the other paraeducator, Jessica, worries because she does not receive clear directions and that she does her own planning for students. She believes that it is not part of her job to plan:

> I'm here to work with the kids, not plan for the kids. I would like things to do with Sarah [the student] but it's hard to think of things, it is not my job. ... I mean we're not paid enough to think of things.

Jessica takes Sarah out of the classroom when she disturbs other students and when she does not know how to involve Sarah in the classroom activities.

The classroom teachers and related service providers have no scheduled planning meetings with Dan either. Sarah's classroom teacher, Julie, does not particularly see the need to meet with Dan because it is her belief that planning for Sarah is either Dan's or the paraeducator's job. Moreover, Julie notes that Sarah does not spend much time in her class due to Sarah's limitations.

Rebecca, another classroom teacher, also names time constraints as the primary problem with scheduling regular meetings but she says, "We definitely do it in a more reactive than proactive way, and I would like to see that changed." She is sympathetic toward Dan's heavy caseload and appreciates that he is trying to do his best to communicate with everyone. Dan does have one formal strategy for communicating with paraeducators about student progress. The paraeducators use a clipboard with a summary of the IEP goals and objectives on which they jot down notes regarding successes or failures in accomplishing goals. However, they do not have specific directions regarding the unit of measurement to use or what kinds of behaviors or performances would be evidence of success or failure.

Keeping with his philosophy of being a partner with parents, Dan tries hard to be there for them. Dan reports that he is always available to the parents and speaks to them whenever there is a reason to talk in person. He maintains a back-and-forth book between school and parents. Dan and the paraeducators write about the students' days at school and send them home with students. The books come back in the morning with parents' notations and comments. Parents consider Dan as the contact or point person regarding questions, concerns, and issues relating to their children. However, one parent bemoans that she often has to call Dan to remind him to get things done.

Analysis of Two Teachers and Five Executive Functions

1. Planning

For a special educator, planning and consultation with other school professionals are equally critical to ensure successful inclusion for students (Friend & Cook, 2003). Although Jamie recognizes that she cannot be well versed in all curricula, she is absolutely clear about the purposes of including students in the classroom. She gathers information from classroom teachers and considers her students' IEP goals in light of the curriculum and instructional style of the teacher. She then prescribes appropriate adaptations and provides written direction and guidance to paraeducators, who carry out the adaptations.

Dan, however, has found no time to meet with teachers to obtain similar information. As a result, he cannot plan adaptations that are specific to the classroom. This results in paraeducators designing instruction or making on-the-spot adaptations, functions that remain outside their legitimate scope of responsibility. The reason that Dan's students are spending more time out of the classroom is that there are no specific instructional and or behavioral plans in place that the classroom teachers and paraeducators can follow to keep the students engaged.

2. Assessment

Dynamic instruction is founded on good planning and good planning is founded on the right assessment information, the basis of planning curricular and instructional adaptations for students with special education needs. Although Jamie and Dan have paper-and-pencil based data collection systems designed to collect information about student experiences and performance in classrooms, there is one critical difference in the two systems. Jamie's system defines exactly what data she requires to determine whether a student is making progress toward an IEP goal. The paraeducators in Jamie's program do not determine the types of data to collect, but are charged with collecting the prescribed data and giving them to her daily. Jamie uses the data to compare to the IEP goals and objectives for the student and to plan adaptations for upcoming classroom activities. The data also provide the basis for parent communications—helping parents stay up to date on their children's progress.

Dan's system is looser, allowing for more individuality in the type of information written by the paraeducators. Because he does not prescribe specific types of data that he wants them to collect, at the end of a week he has little evidence of progress toward IEP goals and little understanding of how special education students are performing in general education classrooms. He has little to use for planning purposes, little to keep him on track with next steps, and few specifics to share with parents.

3. Instruction

Jamie describes herself as being immersed in the classroom, and the general education teachers agree with that characterization. The reality is that she takes time to meet with teachers, related services providers, and paraeducators during the school day. She makes the most of the time she spends in the classroom by working directly with students and assessing how they are doing. She conducts *environmental scans* and evaluates the demands of the classroom so she can devise appropriate adaptations for her students. She also uses her classroom time to observe the work of paraeducators, noting where they need skill development and where they need to be commended for their work.

Dan, in contrast, uses no instructional time for meetings. He spends the majority of his time either in general education classrooms, teaching and assessing students there, or working with individual students in the special education room when they are pulled out. His students are frequently pulled out of classrooms because of disruptions or due to the lack of a plan for their participation in particular activities. His focus tends to remain on the individual child he is working with at the moment. Because he often schedules the paraeducators into different classrooms during this time, he loses the opportunity to observe them so that he can later provide feedback.

4. Collaboration

Experts have emphasized that school reform is evidenced when all stakeholders come together to collaboratively create inclusive classrooms and schools that meet the unique and diverse needs of students (Jackson, Ryndak, & Billingsley, 2000; Rainforth & York-Barr, 1997; Stainback, Stainback, & Forest, 1989). Collaboration with families and across disciplines is not an option but a necessity that is entrenched within the education mandate of the IDEA (Villa, Thousand, Nevin, & Malgeri, 1996). The importance of leadership in establishing collaborative practices has been underscored in the literature (Sarason, 1991; Villa et al., 1996). According to Fisher et al. (2003), "Special educators streamline information, problem solving, accessing materials, strategies and services. Successful special educators are masters of collaboration and skillful negotiators" (p. 46). Jamie models exactly this kind of leadership role in her coordination of collaborative efforts toward inclusion. She ensures that everyone has sufficient information about individualized plans and provides adapted and modified materials and techniques to address IEP goals. She provides accurate and timely information to parents and exchanges ideas with them about how they can collaboratively support their children's education.

Jamie's success as a leader relies on her ability to keep everyone on the same page through formal communication systems and processes that she has established. Her students are successfully included because she communicates, consults, and plans with parents, general education teachers, special education teachers, paraeducators, and related-service providers in an organized manner.

The impromptu, on-the-fly, and often disjointed hallway conversations Dan uses are a less effective and efficient means of communication, problem solving, and conflict management. The best communication systems allow for two-way communication based on student needs, IEPs, and classroom lesson or activity plans (French, 2003).

However, no matter how good a team is at communicating via written plans or other asynchronous means, face-to-face communications in regularly scheduled meetings are absolutely necessary. Jamie uses her school hours to meet with each of the groups of people vitally engaged in the inclusion effort. She facilitates meetings, makes them as brief as possible, and assures that the right topics are addressed and that decisions are documented. Dan, in contrast, believes that collaboration is important, but without specific meetings and communication systems, he cannot make it happen.

5. Supervision of paraeducators

Like Jamie, all special education teachers should assign specific tasks, deliver on-the-job training, hold planning meetings, design instructional plans, and direct and monitor the day-to-day activities of the paraeducators (French, 2003; French & Pickett, 1997). As the supervisor, a special educator must clarify roles and assign tasks based on legal, ethical, and liability considerations, and provide written plans. A good written adaptation plan should include the purpose of the student's participation; IEP goals and objectives to be addressed; student strengths and needs; adapted materials or directions for creating them; and use of cues, prompts, and a data structure for documenting student performance (French, 2003). Effective supervisors do not let paraeducators work on their own. They not only provide written plans, but they also monitor task performance through frequent observations and provide timely, specific feedback. They either provide coaching and on-the-job training or seek outside professional development opportunities for paraeducators to enhance their skills.

Teachers, like Dan, who cannot find the time to write plans for paraeducators are not providing effective supervision. If a teacher is never available to observe and coach a paraeducator in the general education classroom, then he or she is not providing appropriate supervision. If a teacher fails to set up a system by which paraeducators collect student data, he or she cannot effectively evaluate the effects of paraeducator work with students.

The Contrast

We picked these two cases to illustrate the importance of the role of the special education teacher as executive because the two teachers are alike in many ways but differ on one important element. Both are kind, committed teachers of students with similar needs, and both have a genuine commitment to inclusion. Both are energetic, articulate, and creative people who are respected by their colleagues and liked by students' parents. They work in the same school district, and have similar supports available.

Dan, as an early-career teacher, does not yet see himself as an executive—nor does he act like one. He has had no preparation to perform in a leadership capacity. He does not know how to prioritize time for meetings and does not fundamentally understand the importance of doing so. Although everyone at Fox Trail mentions the importance of teamwork and communication, Dan maintains no formalized structures. Dan does not obtain weekly information on curricular activities or units to assist in planning appropriate adaptations for paraeducators. Dan, therefore, fails to guide their work, observe them, or provide them with coaching. In essence, Dan fails to exercise his executive status, resulting in a disjointed approach to inclusion in which well meaning people inadvertently maintain a culture of isolation. The net result is that Dan's students spend more time out of the regular classroom than in.

In contrast, Jamie, a mature teacher, embraces her executive status and her program exemplifies distributed leadership (McNulty & Bailey, 2004). Under her leadership, teamwork is organized—relying on an established schedule of meetings with all stakeholders as well as an established paper-based system for data collection, reporting, and feedback. Jamie honors the skills and knowledge of her team members, builds trust and enthusiasm, and maintains a culture of collaboration. The paraeducators have specific plans from which to work. They receive guidance, feedback, and coaching because Jamie makes the time to observe their work, thus demonstrating skills learned in the course on paraeducator supervision (French, 1999, 2000).

Although differences in Jamie and Dan's career stage and preparation for leadership functions exist, their relative successes with inclusion are predicated on a single factor—the executive role. Perhaps it is not possible for an early-career teacher to perform the executive or leadership functions with the finesse or grace of a mature teacher, but French (2004) suggests

> Acting like a leader is a tall order for a novice teacher. But, as you continue in the profession and grow with it, you will gradually be able to assume the qualities of a leader by learning to perform leadership functions. (p.42)

The shift toward an executive role signifies a corresponding shift to a more professional status. There has been much discussion about whether teaching is a profession and how teacher qualities compare to the qualities of other professionals, but there is agreement that professionals work in situations with a high degree of uncertainty that requires judgment. "Judgment," says Shulman, "is the hallmark of what it is to be a professional" (1998, p. 15). Jamie's story provides strong evidence of professionalism and a powerful illustration of her work as an executive.

Acknowledgments

We have used pseudonyms throughout this article to protect the identity and privacy of research participants.

References

Berliner, D. (1983a). The executive functions of teaching. *Instructor, 93*(2), 28–33, 36, 38, 40.

Berliner, D. C. (1983b). *If teachers were thought of as executives: Implications for teacher preparation and certification.* Paper prepared for the national Institute of Education Conference on State and Local Policy Implications of effective School Research. (ERIC Document Reproduction Service No. ED245357)

Brown, L., Long, E., Udvari-Solner, A., Davis, L., VanDeventer, P., Ahlgren, C., et al. (1989). The home school: Why students with severe intellectual disabilities must attend the schools of their brothers, sisters, friends, and neighbors. *The Journal of the Association for the Severely Handicapped, 14,* 1–7.

Chopra, R. V. (2002). *Parent-paraeducator collaboration in inclusion: Reality and issues.* Unpublished doctoral dissertation, University of Colorado, Denver.

Chopra, R. V., & French, N. K. (2004). Paraeducator relationships with parents of students with significant disabilities. *Remedial & Special Education (RASE), 25,* 240–251.

Falvey, M. A. (1986). *Community-based curriculum: Instructional strategies for students with severe handicaps.* Baltimore: Brookes.

Fisher, D., Frey, N., & Thousand, J. (2003). What do special educators need to know and be prepared to do for inclusive schooling to work? *Teacher Education and Special Education, 26*(1), 42–50.

French, N. K. (1999). Paraeducator Supervision Academy: An outreach project to prepare school professionals to supervise paraeducators. In K. Murray (Ed.), *7th Annual CSPD Conference on Leadership and Change Monograph* (pp. 60–63). Arlington, VA: Office of Special Education Programs and National Association of State Directors of Special Education.

French, N. K. (2000). Preparing school professional to supervise paraprofessionals. In K. Murray (Ed.), *8th Annual CSPD Conference on Leadership and Change Monograph* (pp. 145–150). Arlington, VA: Office of Special Education Programs and National Association of State Directors of Special Education.

French, N. K. (2003). *Managing paraeducators in your school: How to hire, train, and supervise non-certified staff.* Thousand Oaks, CA: Corwin Press.

French, N. K. (2004). Maximizing the services of paraeducators. In J. Burnette, (Ed.), *Thriving as a special education teacher* (pp. 41–48). Arlington, VA: ERIC Clearinghouse on Disabilities and Gifted Education, Council for Exceptional Children.

French, N. K., & Chopra, R. V. (1999). Parent perspectives on the role of the paraeducator in inclusion. *The Journal of the Association for the Severely Handicapped, 24,* 259–272.

French, N. K., & Pickett, A. L. (1997). Paraprofessionals in special education: Issues for teacher educators. *Teacher Education and Special Education, 20,* 61–73.

Friend, M., & Cook, L. (2003). *Interactions: Collaboration skills for school professionals* (4th ed.). Boston: Allyn & Bacon.

Fullan, M. (1990). Staff development, innovation and institutional development. In B. Joyce (Ed.), *Changing school culture through staff development* (pp. 3–25). Alexandria, VA: Association for Supervision and Curriculum Development.

Garman, N. B. (1986). Reflection, the heart of clinical supervision: A modern rationale for practice. *Journal of Curriculum and Supervision, 2*(1), 1–24.

Garmston, R. (1987). How administrators support peer coaching. *Educational Leadership, 44*(5), 18–26.

Garmston, R. (1988, August). A call for collegial coaching. *The Developer,* p. 1, 4–6.

Glatthorn, A. A. (1997). *Differentiated supervision* (2nd ed.). Alexandria, VA: Association for Supervision and Curriculum Development.

Individuals With Disabilities Education Act of 1990, Pub. L. 101-476, 104 Stat. 1103 (1990).

Individuals With Disabilities Education Act Amendments of 1997, Pub. L. No. 105-17, 111 Stat. 37 (1997).

Individuals With Disabilities Education Improvement Act of 2004, Pub. L. No. 108-446, 118 Stat. 2647 (2004).

Jackson, L., Ryndak, D., & Billingsley, F. (2000). Useful practices in inclusive education: A preliminary view of what experts in the field of moderate to severe disabilities are saying. *The Journal of the Association for Persons With Severe Handicaps, 25,* 129–141.

McNulty, B. A., & Bailey, J. A. (2004). McRel's balanced leadership framework: School leadership that works. *Journal for Effective Schools, 3*(1), 17–33.

No Child Left Behind Act of 2001, Pub. L. No. 107-110, 115 Stat. 1425 (2002).

Rainforth, B., & York-Barr, J. (1997). *Collaborative teams for students with severe disabilities: Integrating therapy and educational services.* Baltimore: Brookes.

Sarason, S. (1991). *The predictable failure of school reform: Can we change course before it's too late?* San Francisco, CA: Jossey-Bass.

Shulman, L. S. (1998). *Teaching and teacher education among the professions* [Charles W. Hunt Memorial Lecture]. New Orleans, LA: American Association of Colleges of Teacher Education.

Spillane, J. P., Halverson, R., & Diamond, J. B. (2001). Investigating school leadership practice: A distributed perspective. *Educational Researcher, 30*(3), 22–28.

Stainback, S., Stainback, W., & Forest, M. (1989). *Educating all students in the mainstream of education.* Baltimore: Brookes.

U. S. Department of Education, National Center for Education Statistics. (2005). *Table of instructional aides 1989–2000 by state* [Data file]. Available from http://nces.ed.gov/ccd/bat

Villa, R. A., Thousand, J. S., Nevin, A. I., & Malgeri, C. (1996). Instilling collaboration as a way of doing business in public schools. *Remedial and Special Education, 17,* 169–181.

Jacqueline S. Thousand
Richard A. Villa
Ann I. Nevin

The Many Faces of Collaborative Planning and Teaching

The rationale for and documented benefits of collaborative planning and teaching are explored in this article. When teachers collaborate on their planning and teaching, they are better able to meet the needs of diverse students and fulfill their legal responsibilities. In addition, the authors describe the multiple ways to collaborate and coteach, including working with students as collaborative partners. Readers are provided with answers to some of the frequently asked questions about collaborative planning and coteaching. The authors describe a method for assessing the effectiveness of teaching teams and provide tips for successful collaborative planning and teaching. The importance of professional development and other forms of administrative support are emphasized. The mutual responsibilities of university personnel preparing future teachers, school administrators, and individual educators are discussed.

IN 1994 THE UNITED NATIONS Educational, Scientific and Cultural Organization issued the *Salamanca Statement and Framework for Action on Special Needs Education,* which supported the practice of inclusive education for students with disabilities, with the caution that "while inclusive schools provide a favorable setting for achieving equal opportunity and full participation, their success requires a concerted effort, not only by teachers and school staff, but also by peers, parents, families and volunteers" (p. 11). More than a decade later, North American schools struggle to create inclusive educational experiences for students, even with federal mandates such as the Individuals With Disabilities Education Act of 1990 (reauthorized as the Individuals With Disabilities Education Improvement Act of 2004) and the No Child Left Behind (NCLB) Act of 2001, both of which promote the inclusion of increasing numbers of students with disabilities as full participants in rigorous academic and general education

---

Jacqueline S. Thousand is a Professor at California State University San Marcos. Richard A. Villa is President of Bayridge Consortium, Inc. Ann I. Nevin is Professor Emerita at Arizona State University and a Visiting Professor at Florida International University.

Correspondence should be addressed to Jacqueline S. Thousand, 645 Front St., No. 1108, San Diego, CA 92101. E-mail: jthousan@csusm.edu

curriculum and assessment. NCLB further requires all teachers to demonstrate subject matter competence in all subject areas they teach, encouraging the establishment of collaborative partnerships between highly qualified general educators, who have demonstrated subject-area expertise, and other specialists (e.g., special educators, speech and language pathologists, teachers of English learners, gifted and talented instructors), who have complementary expertise in specialized learning strategies and content. Legal requirements combined with student demographics, then, point to increased collaborative planning and teaching among school personnel attempting to best educate students in compliance with federal mandates.

Documented Benefits of Collaborative Planning and Teaching

What are the documented benefits of collaboration in planning and teaching (i.e., coteaching) for teachers, students, and schools? A recent comprehensive study conducted by Schwab Learning (2003) documented the impact of collaborative partnerships and coteaching in 16 California elementary, middle, and secondary schools in which teachers, administrators, and support staff creatively arranged for every student to receive blended services from Title 1 teachers, reading specialists, special educators, and paraprofessionals. Results included decreased referrals to intensive special education services, increased overall student achievement, fewer disruptive problems, less paperwork, increased number of students qualifying for gifted and talented education services, and decreased referrals for behavioral problems. In addition, teachers reported being happier and not feeling so isolated. This study reinforces the findings of Walther-Thomas's (1997) evaluation of coteaching models in 23 schools across eight school districts. Positive outcomes included improved academic and social skills for low-achieving students, improved attitudes and self-concepts reported by students with disabilities, and more positive peer relationships. Students perceived that these improvements were the result of more teacher time and attention. The coteachers themselves (general and special educator teaching teams) reported professional growth, personal support, and enhanced sense of community within the general education classrooms. The most frequently mentioned drawback was the lack of staff development to learn how to be more effective coteachers.

Coteaching has been documented to be effective for students with a variety of instructional needs, including students with hearing impairment (Compton et al., 1998; Luckner, 1999); learning disabilities (Klingner, Vaughn, Hughes, Schumm, & Elbaum, 1998; Rice & Zigmond, 1999; Trent, 1998; Welch, 2000); high-risk students with emotional disturbance and other at-risk characteristics (Dieker, 1998); language delays (Miller, Valasky, & Molloy, 1998); English-language learners (Bahamonde & Friend, 1999); and students with and without disabilities in secondary classrooms (Mahony, 1997; Weiss & Lloyd, 2002). Welch (2000) showed that students with disabilities and their classmates all made academic gains in reading and spelling on curriculum-based assessments in the cotaught classrooms. Moreover, Mahony (1997) reported that "for special education students [in cotaught classrooms], being part of the large class meant making new friends" (p. 59) in addition to meeting their educational needs.

Coteaching can also result in increased student performance on high-stakes assessments. The Memphis *Commercial Appeal* (Noeth, 2004) reported coteaching being used in all Shelby County, Tennessee high schools, resulting in 70% of the county's special education students being included in general education classrooms through support of teams made up of a special educator and a general education teacher certified in either English or mathematics. After 1 year of coteaching, the percentage of participating special education students passing the Gateway English test increased from 20% to 40%. Due to the test score gains, several high schools were removed from NCLB's troubled schools list.

In summary, there is an emerging database for preschool through high school levels (Villa, Thousand, Nevin, & Malgeri, 1996) that leads to the following conclusions:

1. At all grade levels, students with diverse learning characteristics can be educated effectively in general education environments in which teachers, support personnel, and families collaborate.
2. Improvements are evidenced in academic and social relationship arenas.

What can account for such results? First, coteaching provides a greater opportunity to capitalize on the unique, diverse, and specialized knowledge of each instructor. Second, coteaching allows students to experience and imitate the cooperative and collaborative skills that teachers show when they coteach. With multiple instructors there is increased flexibility in grouping and scheduling, thus making it possible for students to experience less wait time for teacher attention and increased time on task, an important factor documented to increased academic productivity (Kneedler & Hallahan, 1981; Lloyd, 1982; Wheldall & Panagopoulou-Stamatelatou, 1991). Third, teachers who coteach can structure their classes to use more effectively the research-proven strategies required of NCLB (Miller et al., 1998). Fourth, coteaching is a vehicle for bringing together people with diverse backgrounds and interests to share knowledge and skills to generate novel methods to individualize learning. In interviews with 95 peer collaborators and 96 others who were not collaborating, Pugach and Johnson (1995) found that those in the peer-collaboration group had reduced referral rates to special services, increased confidence in handling classroom problems, increased positive attitudes toward the classroom, and more tolerance toward children with cognitive deficits.

What Are the Many Faces of Collaboration and Coteaching?

In some schools, coteaching is incorrectly viewed as the only way to support students with disabilities in inclusive settings. Students eligible for special education can be supported in general education classrooms through a wide variety of collaborative relationships with educators, support personnel, paraprofessionals, and students themselves. Table 1 offers a menu of options for student support that increases in intensity from natural peer supports to individualized supports, including four coteaching approaches, the focus of this article. Individual educational program planning team members, who are responsible for making placement decisions for students with disabilities, are encouraged to review the table and identify the level of support individual students require to receive a free appropriate education in the least restrictive environment. When making support decisions for students to avoid overdependence, team members are encouraged to apply the principle of providing only as much help as necessary. The nature of support for a student may differ from one class or instructional activity to the next. The ultimate goal is to systematically reduce the intensity and frequency of support as students advance in academic and/or social competence.

The authors acknowledge that some students, with and without disabilities, may require support that goes beyond what is typically addressed in any given class (e.g., study skills training, homework support, remediation). To address these support needs, many schools have established learning centers where all students can receive extra support and targeted instruction. Students may be assigned to a learning center during study hall periods or as an alternative to an elective once a day, or they may attend only as long as is necessary for them to master a specific skill. The library media center is an ideal place for a learning center. For example, school personnel at a high school familiar to the authors use the library media center in this way: Every period of every day, one general educator and one special educator are assigned, as an official duty, to work with students in the library media center. In addition to the library media director and the general and special education personnel assigned to the learning center, trained peer tutors are available to provide tutorial and other assistance to their fellow students. Such an arrangement avoids stigmatization of students receiving support and allows all students, whether or not they are eligible for a particular support pro-

Table 1
From Least to Most Intense and Intrusive Student Support Options

Natural peer support	Same-age or cross-age peers can assume responsibility for naturally supporting a student's participation in academic, cocurricular, and social activities. *Natural peer support* includes assisting a student to get from class to class, remember materials, or complete assignments. Peers may take notes for another student, facilitate communication with others unfamiliar with the student's way of communicating (e.g., use of an augmentative communication device), or serve as a role model. Peers also can expand a student's social network by assisting to include the student in free-time interactions, social clubs, and other in-school and out-of-school social activities. Occasionally, a classmate may serve as a peer tutor, providing specific academic instruction.
Consultative and stop-in support	*Consultative support* occurs when one or more adults, often a special educator, meet regularly with classroom teachers to keep track of student progress, assess the need to adapt or supplement materials or instruction, and problem solve, as needed. Specialized professionals such as nurses, occupational and physical therapists, augmentative communication specialists, and guidance or career counselors often provide periodic consultation. Students also may seek assistance from consulting staff for specific assignments or general support. *Stop-in support* occurs when consulting support providers stop by the classroom on a scheduled or unscheduled basis to observe student performance in the general education context, assess the need for any modifications to existing supports or curriculum, and talk face to face with the student, classroom teacher, and peers.
Coteaching support	*Coteaching support* occurs when two or more people share responsibility for teaching some or all of the students assigned to a classroom. There are four predominant coteaching approaches: a) *supportive teaching,* in which one teacher takes the lead and others rotate among students to provide support, b) *parallel teaching,* in which coteachers work with different groups of students in different areas of the classroom, c) *complementary teaching,* in which coteachers do something to enhance the instruction provided by another coteacher, and d) *team teaching,* in which coteachers jointly plan, teach, assess, and assume responsibility for all of the students in the classroom.
Individualized support	*Individualized support* involves one or more adults, oftentimes paraprofessionals, providing support to one or more students at predetermined time periods during the day or week or for most or all of the day. The key to successful individualized support is to ensure that designated support personnel do not become "attached at the hip" to individual students, but, instead, deliberately prompt natural peer support, support students in the class other than the focus student, facilitate small group learning with heterogeneous groups of classmates, and differentiate support, as needed, through planning with the classroom teacher. The ultimate goal is to fade the need for individualized support by facilitating increased student independence and increased natural support from classmates and teachers.

gram, to receive assistance from teachers and peers on an as-needed basis.

What Does Coteaching Look Like? Four Approaches

In a comprehensive national survey, teachers experienced in meeting the needs of students in a diverse classroom reported that they used four predominant coteaching approaches: *supportive, parallel, complementary,* and *team* teaching (National Center for Educational Restructuring and Inclusion, 1995). Before describing each approach in more detail, it is important to point out that none of these four coteaching approaches is better than another. When deciding which approach to use in a given lesson, the goal always is to improve the educational outcomes of students through the selected coteaching approach. Many beginning coteachers start with supportive teaching and parallel teaching because these approaches involve less structured coordination among the coteaching team members. As coteaching skills and relationships strengthen, coteachers then venture into the complementary teaching and team teaching approaches that require more time, coordination, and knowledge of and trust in one another's skills.

Supportive Teaching

Supportive teaching is when one teacher takes the lead instructional role and the other(s) rotates among the students to provide support. The coteacher(s) taking the supportive role watches or listens as students work together, stepping in to provide one-to-one tutorial assistance when necessary, while the other coteacher continues to direct the lesson. A caution in using the supportive teaching approach is that whoever is playing the support role (e.g., special educator, paraprofessional) must not become "velcroed" to individual students, functioning as hovercraft vehicles blocking students' interactions with other students. This can be stigmatizing for students and the support persons, leading students to perceive that the student and support teacher are not genuine members of the classroom.

Parallel Teaching

Parallel teaching is when two or more people work with different groups of students in different sections of the classroom. Parallel teaching includes at least the following eight variations.

1. *Split class.* Each coteacher is responsible for a particular group of students, monitoring understanding of a lesson, providing guided instruction, or reteaching the group, if necessary.
2. *Station teaching or learning centers.* Each coteacher is responsible for assembling, guiding, and monitoring one or more centers or stations.
3. *Coteachers rotate.* The coteachers rotate among two or more groups of students.
4. *Each coteacher teaching a different component of the lesson.* This is similar to station teaching, except that teachers rotate from group to group rather than students rotating from station to station.
5. *Cooperative group monitoring.* Each coteacher takes responsibility for monitoring and providing feedback and assistance to a given number of cooperative groups of students.
6. *Experiment or lab monitoring.* Each coteacher monitors and assists a given number of laboratory groups, providing guided instruction to those groups requiring additional support.
7. *Learning style focus.* One coteacher works with a group of students using primarily visual strategies, another works with a group using auditory strategies, and yet another uses kinesthetic strategies.
8. *Supplementary instruction.* One coteacher works with most of the class on a concept, skill, or assignment. The other coteacher (a) instructs students to apply or generalize the skill to a relevant community environment, (b) provides extra guidance to students who are self-identified or teacher-identified as

needing extra assistance in acquiring or applying the learning, or (c) provides advanced enrichment activities.

As with supportive teaching, there are cautions in implementing parallel teaching. Primarily, there is the possibility of creating a special class within a class by routinely grouping the same students in the same group with the same coteacher. It is important to keep groups heterogeneous whenever possible and to rotate students among different coteachers. Students stretch their learning by experiencing different instructors' approaches and expertise. They avoid stigmatization that may arise if someone other than the classroom teacher (e.g., special educator or paraprofessional) always teaches one set of students. With all members of the coteaching team familiar with all students, teachers are better able to problem solve any barriers to academic, communication, and social learning that their common students encounter.

Complementary Teaching

Complementary teaching is when coteachers do something to enhance the instruction provided by the other coteacher(s). For example, one coteacher might provide a lecture on the content while the other coteacher paraphrases statements and models note-taking on the content on chart paper or a transparency. Sometimes, one of the complementary teaching partners preteaches the small-group social skill roles required for successful cooperative group learning and then monitors as students practice the roles during the academic cooperative group lesson facilitated by the other coteacher. A common concern with complementary teaching, particularly at the secondary level, is that those coteachers who are not the content area teachers do not have the same level of content mastery as the content teacher. This cannot be avoided and is not necessarily a drawback. Complementary teaching partners have expertise in other areas (e.g., speech and language pathologists have expertise in communication, a special educator has expertise in adapting curriculum and learning strategies, a paraprofessional speaks fluent Spanish or another language that is the primary language for many of the students in the classroom) that can be readily used to complement and supplement the expertise of the content area teacher. Through planning and teaching together, all members of the team have an opportunity to acquire new skills. For example, the special educator may learn new content and the classroom teacher may acquire skills to differentiate curriculum, instruction, and assessment.

Team Teaching

Team teaching is when two or more people do what the traditional teacher has always done—plan, teach, assess, and assume responsibility for all of the students in the classroom. Team teachers share the leadership and the responsibilities. For example, one might demonstrate the steps in a science experiment while the other models the recording and illustrating of its results. Coteachers who team teach divide the lessons in ways that allow the students to experience each teacher's strengths and expertise. For example, for a lesson on inventions in science, one coteacher whose interest is history will explain the impact on society. The other coteacher's strengths are more focused on the mechanisms involved and can explain how the particular inventions work. In team teaching, coteachers simultaneously deliver lessons; both teachers are comfortable alternately taking the lead and being the supporter. The bottom line and test of a successful team-teaching partnership is that the students view each teacher as their teacher.

Team teaching is not issue free. One concern is whether team teachers should remain together at the end of the school year or whether one coteacher, such as the special educator, should follow students transitioning to the next grade level. There are advantages and disadvantages both ways. Starting over again every year with a new teaching team can thwart the development of coteaching relationships and content knowledge. On the other hand, there are obvious benefits to teachers receiving new students at risk of failure with accompanying teaching personnel who know the students. The new teacher has immediate access to resource personnel with in-depth knowledge of the student(s). It is up to each team to

Students as Collaborative Partners

Collaborative skills are important to success in 21st-century life. Consequently, one important reason for teachers to collaborate is to allow their students to experience and imitate the cooperative skills teachers demonstrate when they collaboratively plan and teach. Students also can become collaborative partners with their teachers. As explained in Villa, Thousand, & Nevin (2004), students are more likely to develop collaborative dispositions and skills when their teachers explicitly (a) teach them how to tutor or work as study buddies, and (b) structure reciprocity so students serve as teacher and learner. Similarly, by structuring cooperative group learning experiences, teachers create forums for students to practice communication and interpersonal skills while jointly acquiring and demonstrating learning outcomes.

Assessing Collaborative Planning, Teaching, and Learning Relationships

In all collaborative planning, teaching, and learning relationships, there are five elements that facilitate cooperative functioning: *face-to-face interaction, positive interdependence, interpersonal skills, monitoring,* and *individual accountability* (see Johnson & Johnson, 2000, for detailed explanations of each).

For collaborative partners to be optimally effective, they need to know what the five elements of cooperative functioning look like when team members are sitting face to face and planning or debriefing curriculum, instruction, or assessment.

Issues in Collaborative Planning and Teaching

All collaborative planning and teaching teams face common issues concerning instruction, time for planning and other logistics, behavior management, communication among members, and the evaluation of success in collaborating. Among the questions teammates must ask themselves are "Who adapts the curriculum and the instructional and assessment procedures for select students?" "Who carries out the disciplinary procedures and delivers the consequences?" "How will students' progress be monitored?" and "Who completes the paperwork for students eligible for special education?" Some questions relate to daily responsibilities, such as giving feedback on assignments and recording student progress. Others relate to periodically occurring roles such as meeting with parents and administrators. It can be anticipated that answers to many questions will change as members of the team gain experience and trust with one another.

Tips for Success in Collaborative Planning and Teaching

Effective collaborative teachers can achieve more effective outcomes for their students, feel happier about their work, and be more likely to work together in the future (Villa, Thousand, & Nevin, 1999) when they practice the following tips.

1. Know with whom you need to collaborate. Who will be affected by the decisions you make? Who has the expertise? Who wants to participate? Include those who will help you invent new solutions.
2. Establish and clarify collaborative goals to avoid hidden agendas. Goal setting helps each member of the collaborative team achieve what each person needs for success. Creating a common goal sets up a positive interdependence with each other.
3. Agree to use a common conceptual framework, language, and interpersonal skills. Avoid using jargon terms. Participate in staff development and training to learn similar strategies. Establish ground rules to make it OK to ask questions for clarification and to learn from each other.
4. Practice communication skills to concurrently achieve the task and maintain relationships. Consciously include trust building and creative problem-solving activities in collaborative planning. Be sure that absent team

members are notified of decisions. Clarify accountability for who will do what, set deadlines, and include celebrating daily successes.
5. Know how to facilitate a collaborative climate. Changing to a collaborative culture means that unconscious beliefs must be made conscious. For example, new traditions that celebrate cooperation must replace the old traditions of competition. Instead of celebrating one teacher of the year, add a coteacher team award.
6. Recognize and respect differences in motivation of collaborators. Create flexible scheduling to encourage collaborative teachers to use their time to meet and plan as well as debrief and problem solve. Set up multiple opportunities to observe others to discover their secrets of effective collaboration.
7. Expect to be responsible and expect to be held accountable. Support and facilitate individual and team actions such as following through on agreements.
8. Agree to reflective analysis of collaborative planning and celebrate often. Create a tool to measure the changes of collaborative partners (see Thousand & Villa, 2000, for an example). Periodically take time to celebrate the positive changes.

Conclusions: A Triangle of Responsibility

Our task is to teach the kinds of kids we have, not the kinds of kids we used to have, want to have, or the kids that exist in our dreams. (Gerlach, 2002, personal communication)

Collaborative planning and teaching can result in a variety of positive outcomes for the kids we have today as well as the educators who teach these children and youth. Yet we acknowledge that collaborative planning and teaching is intellectually and interpersonally demanding; it has not occurred spontaneously or naturally within most schools.

To achieve the research promise of collaborative teaching requires institutions and individuals to take responsibility at three levels. First, at the university level, teacher preparation institutions must accept the responsibility to provide training in and modeling of effective collaborative planning and teaching practices for all future educators. Second, at the school district level, school administrators must assume responsibility for providing ongoing professional development in collaborative planning, the four approaches to coteaching, differentiated instructional practices, cooperative group and peer tutoring learning, positive behavioral supports, and other best educational practices that support diverse learners to succeed in general education. Administrators also must assume responsibility for (a) articulating the rationale for collaborative planning and teaching, (b) assisting school personnel to understand the necessary changes in their traditional roles and responsibilities, (c) providing incentives and resources for collaborative planning and teaching (e.g., scheduling common planning and teaching time, opportunities to attend conferences and/or observe veteran coteaching teams), and (d) evaluating the efficacy of the collaborative planning and teaching practices at their school sites.

Third, at the individual educator level, it is a fact that the job of *teacher* has become increasingly complex, demanding, and exciting due to our nation's increasingly diverse student population and requirements of NCLB, Individuals With Disabilities Education Improvement Act of 2004, and other state and federal mandates. As professionals who have chosen teaching as a career, we educators have a third tier of responsibility; that is, to take the initiative to keep abreast of the emerging knowledge and skills needed to do the job for which we are paid. We are compelled as professionals to do this regardless of how successful our university teacher preparation programs or school district administrators have been in doing their part to promote collaborative planning and teaching as a natural part of the culture and practice of modern day schooling. After all, collaborative planning and teaching is for the benefit of the kids—the only kids we have.

References

Bahamonde, C., & Friend, M. (1999). Teaching English language learners: A proposal for effective service delivery through collaboration and coteaching. *Journal of Educational and Psychological Consultation, 10*(1), 1–9.

Compton, M., Stratton, A., Maier, A., Meyers, C., Scott, H., & Tomlinson, T. (1998). It takes two: Co-teaching for deaf and hard of hearing students in rural schools. In D. Montgomery (Ed.), *Coming together: Preparing for rural special education in the 21st century: Conference proceedings of the American Council on Rural Special Education.* (ERIC Document Reproduction Service No. 417901)

Dieker, L. (1998). Rationale for co-teaching. *Social Studies Review, 37*(2), 62–65.

Individuals With Disabilities Education Act of 1990, Pub. L. 101-476, 104 Stat. 1103 (1990).

Individuals With Disabilities Education Improvement Act of 2004, Pub. L. No. 108-446, 118 Stat. 2647 (2004).

Johnson, D. W., & Johnson, F. (2000). *Joining together: Group theory and group skills* (7th ed.). Needham Heights, MA: Allyn & Bacon.

Klingner, J., Vaughn, S., Hughes, S., Schumm, J., & Elbaum, B. (1998). Outcomes for students with and without learning disabilities in inclusive classrooms. *Learning Disabilities Research & Practice, 13,* 153–161.

Kneedler, R., & Hallahan, D. (1981). Self-monitoring of on-task behavior with learning disabled children. *Attention Disorders: Implicatons for the Classroom, 2*(3), 73–82.

Lloyd, J. (1982). Reactive effects of self-assessment and self-recording on attention to task and academic productivity. *Learning Disability Quarterly, 5*(3), 216–227.

Luckner, J. (1999). An examination of two co-teaching classrooms. *American Annals of the Deaf, 144*(1), 24–34.

Mahony, M. (1997). Small victories in an inclusive classroom. *Educational Leadership, 54*(7), 59–62.

Miller, A., Valasky, W., & Molloy, P. (1998). Learning together: The evolution of an inclusive class. *Active Learner: A Foxfire Journal for Teachers, 3*(2), 14–16.

National Center for Educational Restructuring and Inclusion. (1995). *National study on inclusive education.* New York: City University of New York.

No Child Left Behind Act of 2001, Pub. L. No. 107-110, 115 Stat. 1425 (2002). Retrieved December 2, 2003, from http://www.ed.gov/policy/elsec/leg/esea02/beginning.html#sec1

Noeth, L. C. (2004, September 9). Co-teaching system boosts special education test scores in Tennessee district. *The Commercial Appeal.* Retrieved September 11, 2004, from http://www.commercialappeal.com/mca/local_news/article/0,1426,MCA_437_3168716,00.html

Pugach, M., & Johnson, L. (1995). Unlocking expertise among classroom teachers through structured dialogue: Extending research on peer collaboration. *Exceptional Children, 62*(2), 101–110.

Rice, D., & Zigmond, N. (1999). *Co-teaching in secondary schools: Teacher reports of developments in Australia and American classrooms* (ERIC Document Reproduction Service No. ED432558).

Schwab Learning. (2003). Collaboratively speaking. A study on effective ways to teach children with learning differences in the general education classroom. *The Special EDge, 16*(3). Retrieved May 18, 2006, from http://www.calstat.org/publications/pdfs/2003sumEinsert.pdf

Thousand, J. S., & Villa, R. A. (2000). Collaborative teams: A powerful tool in school restructuring. In R. A. Villa & J. S. Thousand (Eds.), *Restructuring for caring and inclusive education: Piecing the puzzle together* (pp. 254–291). Baltimore: Brookes.

Trent, S. (1998). False starts and other dilemmas of a secondary general education collaborative teacher: A case study. *Journal of Learning Disabilities, 31*(5), 503–513.

United Nations Educational, Scientific and Cultural Organization. (1994). *The Salamanca statement and framework for action on special needs education.* Geneva, Switzerland: Author. (Document 94/WS/18)

Villa, R., Thousand, J., & Nevin, A. (1999). Eight habits of highly effective collaborators. *Missouri Educational Leadership, 9*(2), 25–29.

Villa, R., Thousand, J., & Nevin, A. (2004). *A guide to co-teaching: Practical tips for facilitating student learning.* Thousand Oaks, CA: Corwin Press.

Villa, R., Thousand, J., Nevin, A., & Malgeri, C. (1996). Instilling collaboration for inclusive schooling as a way of doing business in public education. *Remedial and Special Education, 17*(3), 169–181.

Walther-Thomas, C. (1997). Co-teaching experiences: The benefits and problems that teachers and principals report over time. *Journal of Learning Disabilities, 30,* 395–407.

Weiss, M., & Lloyd, J. (2002). Congruence between roles and actions of secondary special educators in co-taught and special education settings. *Journal of Special Education, 36*(2), 58–68.

Welch, M. (2000). Descriptive analysis of team teaching in two elementary classrooms: A formative experimental approach. *Remedial and Special Education, 21*(6), 366–376.

Wheldall, K., & Panagopoulou-Stamatelatou, A. (1991). The effects of pupil self-recording of on-task behavior on primary school children. *British Educational Research Journal, 17*(2), 113–127.

Diane M. Browder
Shawnee Y. Wakeman
Claudia Flowers

Assessment of Progress in the General Curriculum for Students With Disabilities

Legislative initiatives and federal regulations require states to provide students with disabilities access to the general curriculum and to include all students in state assessment systems. Assessing the progress in the general curriculum for students with disabilities challenges states to determine how academic standards apply to all students and to create universally designed assessments. Decisions regarding the use of accommodations, alternate assessments, and out-of-level testing continue to be discussed and debated. Implications for research include the continued development and use of universally designed assessments and instruction, the alignment of alternate assessments to state standards, an increase in the scope of progress monitoring to include students with significant disabilities, and the promotion of state standard attainment by students through effective teacher practices.

Diane Browder is a Snyder Distinguished Professor in the Department of Special Education & Child Development at the University of North Carolina at Charlotte. Shawnee Wakeman is a Research Associate in the National Alternate Assessment Center at the University of North Carolina at Charlotte. Claudia P. Flowers is Associate Professor of Educational Leadership at the University of North Carolina at Charlotte.

Correspondence should be addressed to Diane Browder, Department of Special Education & Child Development, University of North Carolina at Charlotte, 9201 University City Blvd., Charlotte, NC 28223. E-mail: dbrowder@email.uncc.edu

HAVING ACCESS TO THE GENERAL curriculum is more than being present in inclusive contexts. Full general curriculum access also requires having the opportunity and instructional support to learn the core academic content typical of one's grade level. Being present in general education classrooms increases students' opportunities for exposure to general curriculum content. In contrast, students with more intensive support needs may be less likely to be involved in general curriculum tasks in these settings (Wehmeyer, Lattin, Lapp-Rincker, & Agran, 2003.) This article describes changing expectations for all students to make progress in the general curriculum and the assessments schools use to track this progress for students with disabilities.

Expectations for Progress in the General Curriculum

Defining what is meant by the general curriculum is complicated for at least two reasons. First, the United States is the only major world power without a national curriculum (English & Steffy, 2001). Instead, each state determines priorities for student learning. Thus, there is interstate variation in what is expected in fifth-grade reading, for example. Second, there are a surprising number of meanings assigned to the term *curriculum* (Cuban, 1992). The term *curriculum* may refer to the overall educational program, the textbooks used in the classroom, or the full range of experiences students have in school. In this article we focus specifically on the content to be learned. It is also important to note that the *taught* curriculum is not always the *intended* curriculum. In the past 2 decades, professional organizations and states have defined standards. States typically have academic *content* standards that specify what students should know, and *achievement* standards that specify how students demonstrate mastery of the content. States also typically delineate standards by grade level. Because standards define what students are expected to learn, they provide a focal point for discussion of the general curriculum.

The movement to define standards for all students' learning and to hold schools accountable for this learning through large-scale assessments is called *standards-based reform*. In the early era of standards-based reform, students with disabilities were excluded from assessments and accountability systems. Subsequently, professionals like Thurlow, Elliott, and Ysseldyke (1998) argued for the inclusion of students with disabilities in these large-scale assessments. This inclusion could help schools have an accurate picture of the students' education, avoid the unintended consequences of exclusion, and promote high expectations for all students.

Access to the general curriculum and inclusion in state assessment systems has now been established by legislative mandates and requirements of the Individuals With Disabilities Education Act (IDEA) Amendments of 1997, the Improving America's Schools Act (IASA; 1994, Title 1) and No Child Left Behind (NCLB) Act of 2001. IASA included (a) the mandate of state-developed content and performance standards in language arts and math and (b) the use of an evaluation system that included measures of yearly progress based on student performance on state assessments linked to the state standards. IDEA (1997) required that all students with disabilities have access to the general curriculum and be included in state and district assessments. Students who were unable to participate in large-scale assessments with accommodations were to be given alternate assessments. The final regulations of Title 1, as written by the U.S. Department of Education (2003a), stated that regardless of where students receive instruction, all students with disabilities should have access to, participate in, and make progress in the general curriculum. Last, NCLB required annual performance assessments for all students in reading and math in Grades 3 through 8. These legislative initiatives propelled states to make changes to include all students, including those with disabilities, in curriculum and assessment endeavors.

Not all professionals have agreed with including students with disabilities in the standards-based reform movement. Lashley (2002) argued that these requirements overlook students' previous failure in the general curriculum, the functional needs of the students, and the individual needs and abilities of students not captured by standardized assessments. Agran, Alper, and Wehmeyer (2002) found that special education teachers ranked functional and self-determination skills above academics as a priority for students with severe disabilities. These teachers also did not believe that their students should be held to the same standards as those of their nondisabled peers. Byrnes (2001) surveyed separate special education teachers about their knowledge of the general curriculum and how accessing that curriculum could affect their students. Although teachers reported actively increasing their own familiarity with the curriculum through self-study, they also reported great concern for students dropping out of school and having even more limited school outcomes as a result of a general curriculum focus.

One particular concern is the loss of individualization of instruction and content for students with significant disabilities. For example, individual students may need a focus on individual life skills that are not the focus of the state assessment. Although standards-based reform incorporates the need for assessment of academic standards linked to grade-level content, it does not prevent the inclusion of instruction in functional skills that this population needs. The U.S. Department of Education (2005a) explained that progress on individualized education program (IEP) or functional life goals *should* be measured to report progress to parents and make individualized instructional and support decisions. The Department noted that these types of goals *should not* be used for adequate yearly progress (AYP) determinations because it would be impossible to ensure consistency in judgments about schools and that Title I requires only assessment of reading/language arts, mathematics, and science.

Given the potential pitfalls of including students with disabilities in large-scale assessments, the need exists for ongoing monitoring of the intended and unintended consequences of this inclusion. Quenemoen, Lehr, Thurlow, and Massanari (2001) identified several potential positive consequences, including higher levels of learning and achievement; access to the general education curriculum; opportunities to learn that had previously been denied; meaningful diplomas; and accountability for schools, teachers, and students. They noted that possible unintended consequences include lowered expectations on IEPs to ensure mastery; misinterpretation of achievement results; higher rates of dropout, retention, exemptions, or exclusions; and absenteeism, lower graduation rates, teacher burnout, and cheating. Ysseldyke, Dennison, and Nelson (2003) used reports, focus groups, and survey data to determine if there were positive consequences and found increased participation in assessment, higher expectations and standards for students with disabilities, improved instruction (e.g., access to the general education curriculum, alignment of teaching with state standards, data-based decisions), improved student performance on assessments, improved assessments, improved diploma options, increased general and special education collaboration, and increased communication with parents. Additional research is needed to identify other consequences stakeholders may be experiencing. These experiences may also be changing now that students with disabilities are included in school's NCLB reports on adequate yearly progress.

The reality is that state standards and large-scale assessments were not originally developed to be inclusive of all students. The current challenge is to determine how standards apply to all students and to create universally designed assessments (i.e., designing assessments that are appropriate for the widest range of students). The additional challenge is to identify teaching strategies that make it possible for more students to achieve proficiency in state standards. Some research has indicated that more students with disabilities are achieving proficiency in state standards as time goes by (Thurlow, Wiley, & Bielinski, 2003). These improvements provide promise that students with disabilities may meet the expectation for progress in the general curriculum with improved instruction and educational opportunity.

Given that more students with disabilities may be achieving state standards, the question is whether all students should be expected to be proficient at grade level. A Notice on Proposed Rulemaking on NCLB indicated that states could use alternate achievement standards for students with the most significant cognitive disabilities for no more than 1% of all students (U.S. Department of Education, 2003b). The U.S. Department of Education went further (2003a) and explained that a state may adopt alternate achievement standards through a documented and validated standards-setting process, provided that those standards are aligned with the state's academic content standards, promote access to the general curriculum, and reflect professional judgment of the highest achievement standards possible. Most states are in the process of defining these alternate achievement standards.

The controversial issue is the level of achievement to target for students with disabilities who are not in the 1%, but who are significantly below grade level in their current academic performance (e.g., performing at a first-grade reading level in seventh grade). To help address the assessment needs of these students, the Department of Education recently created a policy establishing modified achievement standards for students with persistent academic disabilities. States can include proficient scores from these assessments in AYP decisions for up to 2% of the tested population. Students who may be included in this 2% are not students with significant cognitive disabilities but those students who are unlikely to reach grade-level achievement in the same time frame as students without disabilities (U.S. Department of Education, 2005b). Final regulations on modified achievement standards will guide states in creating modified achievement standards as well as the assessments measuring these standards. There are many uncertainties currently about these assessments and standards. It will be important that states create valid and accessible assessments aligned closely with state standards as well as finely define participation parameters for students. Practitioners, parents, and other stakeholders will need to understand state guidelines around graduation implications and participation in assessments based on modified achievement standards. Research will also be needed to determine the likelihood of students catching up to grade-level standards as a result of participating in the assessments with modified standards.

To summarize, the expectation is for all students to have access to the academic content for their assigned grade level. For example, a 13-year-old student with disabilities who is in eighth grade will be learning the poetry and other literature typically taught for this grade level. If the student has significant cognitive disabilities and is in the 1% of the population who qualify for alternate achievement standards, or has persistent academic disabilities and is in the 2% of the population who qualify for modified achievement standards, he or she will also be learning this content, but with outcomes that differ from grade-level attainment. For example, the student might select picture symbols to illustrate the main idea of a poem or describe the meaning in a given poem using scaffolded support. In contrast, if the student with disabilities is not in the 1% or 2%, the expectation is to be proficient at grade level in eighth grade language arts. How this proficiency is determined is described next.

Assessments to Determine Achievement of State Standards

In just over a decade, the number of students with disabilities included in state assessments has drastically increased. In the early 1990s, most states included 10% or fewer of their students with disabilities in their assessments; by 1998, most states included over 50% of students with disabilities in their assessments (Thompson & Thurlow, 1999). Today 100% of students with disabilities must be included in states' assessments to meet the requirements of IDEA and NCLB. The Educational Policy Reform Research Institution (EPRRI) conducted a national symposium to focus states' discussions on essential components of inclusive systems. It was hoped that states would revisit basic assumptions and beliefs about their assessment systems. Using information from the EPRRI symposium and previous research, the National Center for Educational Outcomes identified six essential principles of inclusive assessment and accountability systems (Thurlow, Quenemoen, Thompson, & Lehr, 2001). The principles are: (a) all students with disabilities are included in the assessment system; (b) decisions about how students with disabilities participate in the assessment system are clearly articulated; (c) all students with disabilities are included when student scores are publicly reported; (d) the assessment performance of students with disabilities has the same impact on the final accountability index as the performance of other students; (e) there is improvement of the assessment system and the accountability system, through the process of formal monitoring, ongoing evaluation, and systematic training; and (f) every policy and practice reflects the belief that all students must be included in state district assessment and accountability systems.

Accommodations

For students with disabilities participating in general assessments, an important decision to be made is whether or not to use accommodations. Accommodations are changes made in testing materials or procedures that allow students with disabilities to participate in testing programs (Elliott, Braden, & White, 2001). Accommodations can include changes in presentation of directions (e.g., repeat directions), testing material (e.g., use of large bubbles), time allocation (e.g., extended time and frequent breaks), setting (e.g., special lighting), and method of student response (e.g., marking answers in book instead of answer sheet). The goal of accommodation is to accurately measure the student's abilities while eliminating barriers that may interfere with the measurement of ability.

Approved accommodations for students with disabilities vary by state and may include Braille, computer response, dictate-to-scribe, extended time, read-aloud, and test breaks, as well as numerous others. Thurlow and Bolt (2001) found that individual administration of test, dictate-to-scribe, and small-group administration were the three most common forms of accommodation used by states. Thompson, Blount, and Thurlow (2002) conducted a literature review of the effects of testing accommodations. Most of the accommodation research examined the effects of read-aloud, computer administration, and extended time. Read-aloud tended to have positive effects on students' scores in the general assessment. Mixed results were found for the accommodations of computer administration (i.e., four studies found positive effect on student scores and three found no effect) and extended time (i.e., four studies found positive effects and three studies found no effect on student outcome).

Although the use of accommodations can provide students with more appropriate methods of demonstrating performance, several cautions should be noted. First, accommodations should not be used only in testing situations, but in instruction as well. This may address the unfamiliarity some students may have with computer use (Thompson, Thurlow, & Moore, 2003; Thurlow & Bolt, 2001). As limitations of use vary from state to state, it is important that states specifically explain which accommodations will and will not influence the inclusion of student scores (Thurlow, Lazarus, Thompson, & Morse, 2005). Finally, the use of an accommodation does not amend for poor instruction. Thompson et al. (2003) stated that no matter how well a test is designed, or what media is used for administration, students who have not had the opportunity to learn the material will perform poorly.

Alternate Assessments

Students who are unable to participate in general assessments with or without accommodations must participate in the testing program through the use of alternate assessments. The U.S. Department of Education (2003b) defined an alternate assessment as:

> an assessment designed for the small number of students with disabilities who are unable to participate in the regular state assessment even with appropriate accommodations. ... This assessment must be aligned with the state's content standards, must yield results separately in reading and math, and be designed and implemented in a manner that supports the use of the results as an indicator of AYP. (p. 68,699)

Alternate assessments have been developed more recently than the general assessments and the underlying assumptions and technique quality continue to be discussed and debated. There is not yet a consensus about how to construct, administer, or score alternate assessments or how alternate assessment will reflect on the academic achievement for students with disabilities.

Quenemoen, Rigney, and Thurlow (2002) described multiple methods that addressed the collection of alternate assessment data. These methods included a (a) portfolio or collection of student work, (b) IEP- linked body of evidence, (c) performance assessment or direct measures of a student's skill(s), (d) checklist or a list of skills reviewed by persons familiar with the student, and (e) traditional test. States have sometimes considered creating alternate assessments using alternate achievement standards that can be the traditional assessment but may include out-of-level testing (i.e., student assessed using a level of a test developed for students in another grade). As the practice of assessing students using a lower-level form of a test has been controversial (Minnema, Thurlow, Bielinski, & Scott, 2000), the U.S. Department of Education (2005a) has clearly delineated when a state may include the assessment scores in AYP of a student who participates in an off-level test. The nonregulatory guidance for alternate achievement standards clarifies that alternate assessments based on grade-level achievement standards cannot be off grade level assessments, but alternate assessments based on alternate achievement standards can be off grade level if the assessment meets the Title I requirements. As out-of-level testing fails to document progress in the general curriculum for the student's assigned grade level, out-of-level scores can not be considered proficient for AYP under NCLB unless defined as an alternate achievement standard. In contrast, alternate achievement standards may be better defined as a differential expectation for learning grade-level content. That is, an alternate achievement standard focuses on a different type of performance such as the example given earlier of the student using picture symbols to document the themes of a poem in eighth grade.

Proficiency can also be demonstrated using modified achievement standards. As the content for the assessment is the grade-level content, states may prioritize content standards, including prerequisite skills to be included in the assessment using modified achievement standards. Students may demonstrate proficiency over fewer test items that may be in a simplified format or broken down into steps. For example, a seventh-grade student may have a reading comprehension passage from *Swiss Family Robinson* (Guillot, 1997 as adapted from Wyss, 1812) using high-interest, low-vocabulary words. The assessment may include two questions of potentially lower cognitive demand from this shortened passage related to the characters and the main idea.

It is also important to understand that alternate assessments can be used for students to demonstrate proficiency *on grade level*. There is no limit on the number of students for whom this alternative can be applied. For example, a student with complex physical challenges might use a portfolio to demonstrate proficiency on fifth-grade academic content standards. In such a case, the student would clearly be reading and performing other skills at the typical fifth-grade level. Not all states use on-grade-level alternate assessments. It also is anticipated that few will use out-of-grade-level assessments given the federal guidelines for alternate achievement standards. States are also currently creating and evaluating assessments using modified achievement standards. In contrast, all states use some form of alternate assessment in general and most are applying alternate achievement standards for some students.

Although most states' large-scale assessments focus on student performance for evaluating student proficiency, alternate assessments may use multiple criteria that include student and educational program variables. Student performance may include number of items correct, level of independence, and ability to generalize. Educational program variables may include how well tasks link to state standards, age appropriateness of tasks, and general program quality such as whether students have opportunities to participate in general education settings, assistive technology, and opportunities for self-determination (Thurlow, in press).

Alignment of Standards and Assessments

If standards indicate the expectations for students and assessments measure those expectations, there should be a high degree of alignment between the two. Alignment is defined as the degree of agreement between standards and assessments. NCLB (Sections 200.2–200.3; 2002) described several dimensions of alignment. First, the assessment should cover the full range of specified state academic content standards. Second, the assessment should measure the content and process aspects of the academic content standards. The assessment should reflect the full range of cognitive complexity and level difficulty as that of the standards. Finally, the assessment results should represent all achievement levels specified in the grade-level, modified, or alternate achievement standards.

Procedures for evaluating the alignment of standards and assessments are available, and research into the effectiveness of these alignment procedures is still emerging (Porter, 2002; Webb, 1997). Alignment procedures for alternate assessments introduce challenges not seen in the general assessments. Some states' alternate assessment procedures (29%) provide specific skills that are to be assessed on the alternate assessments, whereas other states (59%) provide optional examples of skills (Cook, Eignor, & Cahalan, 2004). In some states, alternate assessments within the state vary from student to student, with teachers selecting the content based on the individual student's needs. These variations add to the level of complexity for alignment. Alignment statistics provide evidence of the technical adequacy of alternate assessments. By considering not only whether each item matches a state standard, but also the depth of knowledge and breadth of standards addressed, a more complete picture of alignment can be obtained.

The results of an alignment study of three states' alternate assessments indicate that alternate assessments can be aligned to academic content standards but may capture only a narrow range and depth of the content standards (Flowers, Browder, & Ahlgrim-Delzell, in press). Similarly, many general education assessments, which typically have more items, do not meet an acceptable alignment level (Webb, 1999; Webb 2002; Webb, Horton, & O'Neal, 2002). More research is needed to determine how to align alternate assessments to state standards, especially given the permissibility for using alternate achievement standards. For example, will states use fewer standards, less breadth or depth of standards, or simplify the cognitive challenge in creating these alternate achievement standards?

At the individual student level, alignment is important to ensure that the student has the opportunity to learn the material to be assessed. Students who only receive exposure to grade-level content with most direct instruction focused on remedial or functional skills will not be likely to demonstrate proficiency, even with alternate achievement standards. The educational team needs to plan how to ensure that the student will participate fully in the general curriculum and have ongoing opportunities to demonstrate new learning.

Next Steps for Research and Practice

Universal Design

As mentioned earlier, one of the challenges of including students with disabilities in standards-based reform is that most state standards and most large-scale assessments were not developed to be inclusive of all students. Educators have begun working toward universally designed assessments. *Universal design* is a concept that began in the field of architecture and has developed into creating access for students with disabilities across the field of education, including instruction and assessment. Universal design is a way of providing flexible materials that accommodate individuals with wide variations in sensory, learning, and physical abilities (Orkwis, 2003). Thompson, Johnstone, and Thurlow (2002) define universally designed assessments as ones that are developed from the beginning (i.e., not retrofitting design principles to existing assessments) to allow the participation of a wide range of students and to result in valid inferences about student performance.

Universally designed assessments could have the potential for multiple positive consequences. These assessments may eliminate irrelevant barriers to performance like confusing page layouts or the use of examples not typical for students with certain types of disabilities. Procedures may also be developed (e.g., computerized formats) in which more students can participate with few or no accommodations. Universally designed assessments may benefit other populations such as students with linguistic diversity or those whose native culture differs widely from mainstream U.S. culture if developed to have culturally inclusive items.

Improving Technical Quality and Alignment of Alternate Assessments

Besides the need for large-scale assessments to have universal design features, the alternate assessments to be used must also have adequate technical quality for scores to be a meaningful part of school accountability. A challenge for technical quality remains in the variety of instruments used, the inclusion of multiple individual skills by student, and the multiple criteria for scoring alternate assessments. Guidance is needed for how to establish valid and reliable alternate assessment scores.

The alignment of alternate assessments also represents a significant task. As states plan and conduct alignment studies using acceptable alignment models (e.g., Webb's four criteria, 1997), there is little empirical research in this area. Browder et al. (2004) asked general education curriculum experts, experts in severe disabilities, and stakeholders the extent to which alternate assessment content aligned with academic and functional curricula. Outcomes demonstrated that some states had strong links in reading and math, some states had weak links, and some states had a combination of both. Because academic standards for students with significant disabilities are a fairly new concept, content expectations in reading, writing, math, and science have only recently emerged. The alignment of these expectations with assessments must be accomplished.

Promoting Attainment of State Standards

There is a body of research that recognizes the influence of instruction and the teacher on student achievement (Allinder, 1995; Brophy, 1987; Darling-Hammond, 2000; Hancock, Mayring, Glaeser-Zikuda, Nichols, & Jones, 2000). One underlying presumption of assessment is that effective teaching—not assessment—promotes student performance and growth (Boundy, 2000; Browder & Spooner, 2003; Fuchs & Fuchs, 2004; Thompson, Johnstone, et al., 2002). Students with disabilities must have access to the general curriculum if they are to be successful in making progress toward state content and performance standards.

The development of assessments must provide stakeholders with student progress information so that effective interventions may be developed. When describing the development of alternate assessment goals and evidence, Browder and Spooner (2003) recommended that teachers define specific skills for instruction, set up data collection systems to track progress, incorporate assessment into instruction, and communicate outcomes to stakeholders. Fuchs and Fuchs (2004) lay out the clear benefits of the various elements of curriculum-based measurement for evaluating data and designing and redesigning instructional programs for students. As large-scale assessments potentially carry increased consequences for students and teachers, the evaluation of assessment data must be an ongoing practice throughout the instructional process.

Finally, as research has documented a lack of support by teachers for student access to the general curriculum (Agran et al., 2002; Byrnes, 2001) and the need for an inclusive curriculum (Hitchcock, Meyer, Rose, & Jackson, 2002; Thurlow et al., 1998), there is a need for more information on evidence-based practices that are acceptable and useable by practitioners. Teachers need effective practices that they can incorporate into their instruction to help create access for students with disabilities.

In summary, the inclusion of students in the standards-based reform movement has the potential to increase expectations for learning grade-level academic content. For this potential to be realized, several directions are needed. First, the assessment system needs to be revised to be inclusive of all students. Second, alternate assessments need to be clearly aligned to state academic content standards and have documented technical quality. Third, new teaching strategies are needed to help students make progress in the general curriculum, and this progress should be monitored on an ongoing basis. As these new directions unfold, educators can promote best practice by making careful decisions about how the student will participate in the state assessment (e.g., with or without accommodations or with alternate assessment) and by being sure that the educational program provides the content students will need to meet grade-level standards.

References

Agran, M., Alper, S., & Wehmeyer, M. (2002). Access to the general curriculum for students with significant disabilities: What it means to teachers. *Education and Training in Mental Retardation and Developmental Disabilities, 37,* 123–133.

Allinder, R. M. (1995). An examination of the relationship between teacher efficacy and curriculum-based measurement and student achievement. *Remedial & Special Education, 16,* 247–254.

Boundy, K. (2000, April). Including students with disabilities in standards based education reform. *TASH Newsletter,* 4–5, 21.

Brophy, J. (1987). Teacher effects research and teacher quality. *Journal of Classroom Interaction, 22,* 14–23.

Browder, D. M., & Spooner, F. (2003). Understanding the purpose and process of alternate assessment. In D. Ryndak & S. Alper (Eds.), *Curriculum and instruction for students with significant disabilities in inclusive settings* (pp. 51–72). Needham Heights, MA: Allyn & Bacon.

Browder, D. M., Flowers, C., Ahlgrim-Delzell, L., Karvonen, M., Spooner, F., & Algozzine, R. (2004). The alignment of alternate assessment content to academic and functional curricula. *Journal of Special Education. 37,* 211–223.

Byrnes, M. (2001, April). *Teachers' perspectives about adopting statewide curriculum frameworks for students in out-of-district day and residential special education programs: Reflections on the way to realizing the promise.* Paper presented at the Annual Meeting of the American Educational Research Association, Seattle, WA.

Cook, L., Eignor, D., & Cahalan, C. (2004, June). *Alternate assessments: Key issues and research implications.* Paper presented at the Council of Chief State School Officers Large-Scale Assessment Conference, Boston, MA.

Cuban, L. (1992). Why some reforms last: The case of kindergarten. *American Journal of Education, 100,* 166–194.

Darling-Hammond, L. (2000). Teacher quality and student achievement: A review of state policy evidence. *Education Policy Analysis Archives, 8*(1). Retrieved February 22, 2005, from http://epaa.asu.edu/epaa/v8n1

Elliott, S. N., Braden, J. P., & White, J. L. (2001). *Assessing one and all.* Arlington, VA: Council of Exceptional Children.

English, F. W., & Steffy, B. E. (2001). *Deep curriculum alignment: Creating a level playing field for all children on high-stakes tests of educational accountability.* Lanham, MD: Scarecrow Press.

Flowers, C., Browder, D. M., & Ahlgrim-Delzell, L. (2006). An analysis of three states' alignment between language arts and mathematics standards and alternate assessment. *Exceptional Children, 72,* 201–215.

Fuchs, L. S., & Fuchs, D. (2004). *What is scientifically-based research on progress monitoring?* Washington, DC: National Center on Student Progress Monitoring. Retrieved February 9, 2005, from http://www.studentprogress.org

Guillot, M. (1997). *Swiss Family Robinson.* Oakdale, NY: Edcon Publishing (Original work by Johann Wyss published 1812).

Hancock, D. R., Mayring, P., Glaeser-Zikuda, M., Nichols, M. D., & Jones, J. (2000). The impact of teacher instructional strategies and student anxiety levels on students' achievement in eighth grade German and U.S. classrooms. *Journal of Research and Development in Education, 33,* 232–240.

Hitchcock, C., Meyer, A., Rose, A., & Jackson, R. (2002, July). *Access, participation, and progress in the general curriculum.* Paper presented at the National Capacity Building Institute on Access to the General Curriculum, Arlington, VA.

Improving America's Schools Act of 1994, 20 U.S.C. § 1111 et seq.

Individuals With Disabilities Education Act Amendments of 1997, Pub. L. No. 105-17, 111 Stat. 37 (1997).

Lashley, C. (2002). Participation of students with disabilities in statewide assessments and the general education curriculum: Implications for administrative practice. *Journal of Special Education Leadership, 15,* 10–16.

Minnema, J., Thurlow, M., & Bielinski, J., & Scott, J. (2000). *Past and present understanding of out-of-level testing: A research synthesis* (Out-of-Level Testing Project Report 1). Minneapolis: University of Minnesota, National Center on Educational Outcomes. Retrieved February 9, 2005, from http://education.umn.edu/nceo/OnlinePubs/OOLT1.html

No Child Left Behind Act of 2001, Pub. L. No. 107-110, 115 Stat. 1425 (2002).

Orkwis, R. (2003). *Universally designed instruction.* Washington, DC: Office of Special Education Programs. (ERIC Document Reproduction Service No. ED 475386)

Porter, A. C. (2002). Measuring the content of instruction: Uses in research and practice. *Educational Researcher, 31*(7), 3–14.

Quenemoen, R., Lehr, C. A., Thurlow, M. L., & Massanari, C. B. (2001). *Student with disabilities in standards-based assessment accountability systems: Emerging issues, strategies, and recommendations* (Synthesis Report 37). Minneapolis: University of Minnesota, National Center on Educational Outcomes. Retrieved February 3, 2005, from http://education.umn.edu/NCEO/OnlinePubs/Synthesis37.html.

Quenemoen, R., Rigney, S., & Thurlow, M. (2002). *Use of alternate assessment results in reporting and accountability systems: Conditions for use based on research and practice* (Synthesis Report 43). Minneapolis: University of Minnesota, National Center on Educational Outcomes. Retrieved June 20, 2002, from http://education.umn.edu/NCEO/OnlinePubs/Synthesis43.html

Thompson, S., Blount, A., & Thurlow, M. (2002). *A summary of research on the effects of test accommodations: 1999 through 2001* (Technical Report 34). Minneapolis: University of Minnesota, National Center on Educational Outcomes. Retrieved November 14, 2003, from http://education.umn.edu/NCEO/OnlinePubs/Technical34.html

Thompson, S., Johnstone, C. J., & Thurlow, M. L. (2002) *Universal design applied to large scale assessments* (Synthesis Report 44). Minneapolis: University of Minnesota, National Center on Educational Outcomes. Retrieved February 9, 2005, from http://education.umn.edu/NCEO/OnlinePubs/Synthesis44.html

Thompson, S., & Thurlow, M. (1999). *1999 state special education outcomes: A report on state activities at the end of the century.* Minneapolis: University of Minnesota, National Center on Educational Outcomes. Retrieved February 19, 2005, from http://education.umn.edu/NCEO/OnlinePubs/99StateReport.htm

Thompson, S. J., Thurlow, M. L., Johnstone, C. J., & Altman, J. R. (2005). *2005 state special education outcomes: Steps forward in a decade of change.* Minneapolis, MN: University of Minnesota, National Center on Educational Outcomes. Retrieved November 15, 2005, from http://education.umn.edu/NCEO/OnlinePubs/2005StateReport.htm/

Thompson, S., Thurlow, M., & Moore, M. (2003). *Using computer-based tests with students with disabilities* (Policy Directions No. 15). Minneapolis: University of Minnesota, National Center on Educational Outcomes. Retrieved November 14, 2003, from http://education.umn.edu/nceo/OnlinePubs/Policy15.htm

Thurlow, M., & Bolt, S. (2001). *Empirical support for accommodations most often allowed in state policy* (Synthesis Report 41). Minneapolis: University of Minnesota, National Center on Educational Outcomes. Retrieved February 9, 2005, from http://education.umn.edu/NCEO/OnlinePubs/Synthesis41.html

Thurlow, M. L., Elliott, J. L., & Ysseldyke, J. E. (1998). *Testing students with disabilities: Practical strategies for complying with district and state requirements.* Thousand Oaks, CA: Corwin Press.

Thurlow, M. L., Lazarus, S. S., Thompson, S. J., & Morse, A. B. (2005). State policies on assessment participation and accommodations for students with disabilities. *The Journal of Special Education, 38,* 232–240.

Thurlow, M., Quenemoen, R., Thompson, S., & Lehr, C. (2001). *Principles and characteristics of inclusive assessment and accountability systems* (Synthesis Report 40). Minneapolis: University of Minnesota, National Center on Educational Outcomes. Retrieved December 7, 2001, from http://education.umn.edu/NCEO/OnlinePubs/Synthesis40.html

Thurlow, M., Wiley, H. I., & Bielinski, J._(2003). *Going public: What 2000–2001 reports tell us about the performance of students with disabilities* (Technical Report 35). Minneapolis: University of Minnesota, National Center on Educational Outcomes. Retrieved February 22, 2005, from http://education.umn.edu/NCEO/OnlinePubs/Technical35.htm

U.S. Department of Education. (2003a). Title 1 – Improving the Academic Achievement of the Disadvantaged; Final Rule, 68 Fed. Reg. 236 (December 2, 2002) (codified at 34 C.F.R. pt. 200)

U.S. Department of Education. (2003b). Title I – Improving the Academic Achievement of the Disadvantaged; Proposed Rule, 68 Fed. Reg. 13,797–13,798.

U.S. Department of Education. (2005a). *Alternate achievement standards for students with the most significant cognitive disabilities.* Retrieved August 12, 2005, from http://www.ed.gov/policy/elsec/guid/altguidance.doc

U.S. Department of Education. (2005b). *Raising achievement: Alternate assessments for students with disabilities.* Retrieved August 26, 2005, from http://www.ed.gov/policy/elsec/guid/raising/alt-assess-long.html

Webb, N. L. (1997). *Research Monograph No. 6: Criteria for alignment of expectations and assessments in mathematics and science education.* Washington, DC: Council of Chief State School Officers.

Webb, N. L. (1999). *Alignment of science and mathematics standards and assessments in four states.* (NISE Research Monograph No. 18). Madison, WI/Washington, DC: University of Wisconsin–Madison, National Institute for Science Education/Council of Chief State School Officers.

Webb, N. L. (2002). *Alignment study in language arts, mathematics, science, and social studies of state standards and assessments for four states.* Washington, DC: Council of Chief State School Officers.

Webb, N. L., Horton, M., & O'Neal, S. (2002, April). *An analysis of the alignment between language arts standards and assessments for four states.* Paper presented at the meeting of the American Educational Research Association, New Orleans, LA.

Wehmeyer, M. L., Lattin, D. L., Lapp-Rincker, G., & Agran, M. (2003). Access to the general curriculum of middle school students with mental retardation: An observational study. *Remedial & Special Education, 24,* 262–272.

Ysseldyke, J., Dennison, A., & Nelson, R. (2003). *Large-scale assessment and accountability systems: Positive consequences for students with disabilities* (Synthesis Report 51). Minneapolis: University of Minnesota, National Center on Educational Outcomes. Retrieved August 28, 2005, from http://education.umn.edu/NCEO/OnlinePubs/Synthesis51.html\

Alfredo J. Artiles
Nancy Harris-Murri
Dalia Rostenberg

Inclusion as Social Justice: Critical Notes on Discourses, Assumptions, and the Road Ahead

The purpose of this article is to discuss critically the idea of inclusion as social justice. The authors outline the multiple discourses on inclusion and the disparate meanings of social justice that permeate the inclusive education literature. They assume that greater conceptual clarity will strengthen ongoing reform efforts and help educators understand better the intersection of inclusion and social justice in educational systems that serve culturally and linguistically diverse (CLD) students. A more comprehensive treatment of the idea of inclusive education as social justice will enable educators to prevent the historical inequities that have affected CLD students.

O NE OF THE MOST IMPORTANT developments in contemporary special education is the inclusive education movement. Although inclusion has had a significant impact on policy, research, and practice, it has multiple meanings that range from mere placement of students with disabilities in a general education classroom to the transformation of the philosophy, values, and practices of entire educational systems. Most experts agree that inclusive education should focus on the transformation of educational systems and the justification for such an ambitious project is often based on ideals of social justice (Lipsky & Gartner, 1996). Specifically, it is argued that students with disabilities were historically excluded from opportunities to be educated alongside their nondisabled peers, had been denied access to the general education curriculum, and were educated in programs with little ac-

---

Alfredo J. Artiles is Professor of Curriculum & Instruction at Arizona State University. Nancy Harris-Murri and Dalia Rostenberg are Graduate Research Assistants of Curriculum & Instruction at Arizona State University.
 Correspondence should be addressed to Alfredo J. Artiles, Curriculum & Instruction, Arizona State University, Tempe, AZ 85287. E-mail: Alfredo.Artiles@asu.edu

countability. Therefore, inclusive education is needed as a means to achieve social justice for students with disabilities.

The purpose of this article is to analyze critically the idea of inclusion as social justice. Due to the multiple conversations about inclusion and the disparate meanings of social justice permeating inclusive education efforts, we must refine the conceptualization of these notions to better inform ongoing reform efforts. We hope that greater conceptual clarity will help educators address the rarely examined intersection of inclusion and social justice, particularly to prevent the historical inequities that have affected culturally and linguistically diverse (CLD) students.

We used Dyson's (1999) discussion on the discourses of inclusion to frame the analysis of social justice. He distinguished between the *justification* and the *implementation* discourses on inclusion. The *justification* discourse offers the reasons for an inclusive educational system, whereas the *implementation* discourse focuses on ways inclusive models are carried out. According to Dyson, the *justification* discourse takes two forms, namely (a) the rights and ethics discourse, and (b) the efficacy discourse. In turn, the *implementation* discourse uses either political or pragmatic arguments. In the next section we define these discourses and outline their underlying views of social justice. We comment throughout the article about students from CLD backgrounds and conclude with a critique of conceptions and assumptions of inclusion as social justice and implications for the future of the field.

Discourses of Inclusion

Justification of Inclusion Discourse

A sizable literature has been produced on inclusive education in the past 20 years. Most of the early work focused on a justification for inclusion. These discussions relied on claims about the rights of people with disabilities to a free and appropriate education (Artiles, Trent, & Palmer, 2004). Inclusion's *rights and ethics* discourse calls attention to the roles schools play in reproducing inequalities, particularly for students with disabilities (Dyson, 1999). Although schools were expected to enhance life opportunities and contribute to the creation of a more equitable society, the rights and ethics discourse proponents argued that schools were in fact maintaining societal inequities. This state of affairs was particularly evident for students with disabilities because they were, and continue to be, segregated from mainstream educational activities by virtue of the design of special education as a parallel system. Although the original impetus for the creation of special education was to serve a neglected population, in reality special education's separate location perpetuated the mainstream educational system's refusal to work with a wider range of human abilities. The *rights and ethics* discourse states that the existence of a dual educational system prevents systemic changes to make education responsive to an increasingly diverse society. Similarly, the existence of parallel educational systems privileges professional groups (e.g., school psychologists, special educators) that control specific areas of expertise, which in turn affords them privileged positions and compels them to resist inclusion efforts. Endorsers of this discourse conclude that decisions about special education placement are inevitably linked to questions of rights and ethics because the consequences of such decisions bear on a person's status as marginalized, and shape his or her access to educational opportunities.

An alternative discourse that justifies the need for inclusive education is called the *efficacy* discourse (Dyson, 1999). *Efficacy* discourse critiques segregated models on the grounds of special education's failure to promote student learning. Research is cited to show that students placed in segregated special education programs do not perform significantly better than their peers placed in general education classrooms. The *efficacy* discourse argues that well implemented inclusive education models have social benefits for all (nondisabled and disabled) students. Through well implemented models, inclusion can enhance a student's sense of belonging through participation in contexts in which multiple types of difference are observed, and a community approach toward learning is used (Johnson, 2004). A related critique in the *efficacy* discourse is the lack of impact and differentiation in the organization of teaching and learning in segregated special education programs. Research conducted in the 1970s and 1980s suggested instructional models and interventions across disability programs (i.e., mental retardation, learning disabilities, emotional–behavioral disturbances) did not differ significantly and had a weak impact. Why, it was asked, should we maintain such a costly segregated system of special education if the interventions offered in such settings do not seem to be efficacious? However, the evidence of these issues was mixed.

The Implementation of Inclusion Discourse

In addition to the justification discourses, this literature also focuses on the *implementation* of inclusion (Dyson, 1999). One set of arguments can be characterized as *political* because it is assumed that the transition from a traditional special education system, parallel to general education, to an inclusive system requires political work and struggle. Professional groups (e.g., school psychologists, special and general educators) involved in the traditional special education system might want to maintain the system's structures for particular reasons or gains (e.g., access to resources, control of bureaucratic processes). Thus, this type of *implementation* discourse asserts that the promotion of an inclusive education system requires political actions to address inequitable conditions that affect oppressed individuals or groups (i.e., students with disabilities). Similarly, building an inclusive education system might call for coordinated political actions with other oppressed groups in society (e.g., poor communities, racial minorities). The *implementation* discourse also questions underlying ideas and assumptions that sustain a segregated special education system, such as the assumption that disability is a condition located within the individual that requires differentiated services by personnel with specialized skills.

An alternative discourse concerned with the *implementation* of inclusion is labeled *pragmatic* (Dyson, 1999). This literature focuses on the very nature of inclusive schools and it includes descriptions of the unique organizational traits of such schools (e.g., philosophical values of programs, governance structures, school climate, curricula, pedagogical practices, professional development). Scholars in this tradition have theorized differences between inclusive and traditional schools (Skrtic, 1991) and produced practical guidelines for the implementation of inclusive education practices from school or classroom perspectives (Ainscow, 1994; Udvari-Solner, 1995). Lipsky and Gartner (1998) called for a system grounded in the day-to-day practices of inclusion. These practices include placing students first, providing adequate materials and support, collaborating of key personnel to provide effective instruction, and having a vision for inclusion (Lipsky & Gartner, 1998; Vaughn & Schumm, 1995).

It should be noted that the differentiation of inclusion discourses is artificial because there are complex interactions among them. A common theme across these discourses is the underlying assumption that inclusion serves social justice goals. Interestingly, as in the case of inclusion, there are disparate views of social justice. We summarize these views in the next section.

Social Justice Views in Inclusion Discourses

Special education has traditionally focused on the individual. This is reflected in the fact that disability definitions provide descriptions of individual traits and characteristics. Therefore, it is not surprising that a view of social justice based on the individual has dominated the special education field. Social justice views can be classified as *individualistic* or *communitarian*; both perspectives permeate the discourses on inclusion (see Figure 1).

One of the most prominent individualistic views of social justice emphasizes *access* and *distribution* of resources (Rawls, 1971). From this perspective, societies should allow an unequal distribution of resources "only to the extent that the weakest member of society benefits by that inequality" (Christensen & Dorn, 1997, p. 183). This logic allows for a redistribution of resources

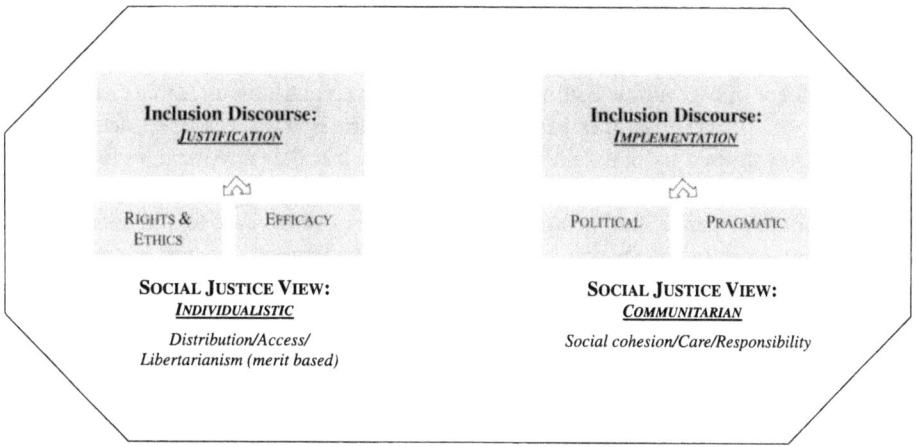

Figure 1. Inclusion discourses and underlying social justice views.

so that underprivileged members of communities can achieve equality. This principle underlies special education and compensatory education.

The discourse on the *justification* for inclusion is based on a distributive view of social justice. As explained previously, this discourse advanced arguments based on individual rights and ethics: "Exclusion of some children from any form of education based on identifiable physical condition and the segregation of others in separate schools and classrooms violate their fundamental human rights" (Christensen, 1996, pp. 68). The proposed solution is to *redistribute* resources by giving access to students with disabilities to the mainstream education system, particularly in light of the lack of efficacy of traditional special education models (Lipsky & Gartner, 1996). Although the discourse to justify inclusion (whether it is concerned with rights issues or the efficacy of special education) focuses on the entire special education system, its underlying view of social justice is individualistic because such discourse is ultimately concerned with individual achievement.

An alternative view of social justice that privileges the individual is *libertarianism* (Christensen & Dorn, 1997). In this view, social justice is based on individual merit. Thus, redistributive policies are not a viable solution because individuals are entitled to the outcomes of their labor; that is, market forces and competition should rule society's handling of social justice. Schools are increasingly based on an individual merit approach as educational achievement and failure are seen as the result of individuals' efforts and ability; as long as students have opportunity to compete, failure is therefore interpreted as an individual outcome (Varenne & McDermott, 1999). As Rizvi and Lingard (1996) explained, "social justice is no longer 'seen as linked to past group oppression and disadvantage' judged historically, but represented simply as a matter of guaranteeing individual choice under the conditions of a 'free market'" (p. 15). For instance, the merit-based perspective hinders analyses and remedies to reduce the disproportionate representation of racial minority students, even in inclusive programs, because student achievement is seen as a purely individual outcome. Issues related to systemic constraints on minority students' opportunities to learn (e.g., these students attend schools where there is a lower teacher quality, higher teacher attrition, and underfunding) tend to be ignored. This situation will not change in the foreseeable future because although special education does not explicitly endorse a merit-based perspective, "most of the [basic principles] of special education law have left intact the meritocratic nature of schools" due to its overreliance on individualistic philosophies (Christensen & Dorn, 1997, p. 187).

In contrast, the discourses on the *implementation* of inclusion (political and pragmatic) draw mostly from a *communitarian* social justice model. A *communitarian* vision favors social cohesion as reflected in values and beliefs that are embraced by members of a group or community (Christensen & Dorn, 1997). From this perspective, social justice is achieved by maintaining responsibilities and rights in a symmetrical relationship. The *political* and the *pragmatic* inclusion discourses seem to emphasize a communitarian vision. In the case of the *political* discourse, the community of people with disabilities is expected to coalesce around a vision of inclusion and build alliances (as needed) with other communities that hold similar values. The goal is to embrace an inclusive vision of education and engage in political struggles that will help build such vision. Similarly, the *pragmatic* discourse requires that schools and educational systems create cohesive organizational cultures guided by inclusive values and practices. Agreed-on inclusion ideals and values should regulate educational opportunities.

In conclusion, multiple perspectives on social justice permeate inclusion discourses. What are the limits of the various visions of social justice and what are the implications for inclusive education models? We reflect on these questions in the next section.

A Critique of Conceptions and Assumptions

Individualistic models of social justice play a central role in inclusion discourses. The *justification* for inclusion discourses use a distributive logic primarily concerned with access and distribution of resources as the way to achieve equality (Rawls, 1971). However, the *distributive* view of social justice has several significant limitations (Young, 1990). First, it does not acknowledge the social contexts in which individuals function in society. It is critical to recognize that individuals do not act in a vacuum, particularly in highly stratified societies like the United States, in which social class, race, gender, and language background (among other markers) afford (or constrain) people's access to participate or secure resources in institutional contexts. Furthermore, greater access and redistribution of resources or freedom to compete do not transform the historically rooted conditions and structures that created the inequalities in the first place. Hence, access does not necessarily translate into meaningful or equal participation. For instance, although more resources have been distributed to students with disabilities than a generation ago and a significantly greater proportion of this population has access to regular schools, we still find minority students with disabilities receiving fewer resources and placed in more segregated programs than their White counterparts (Artiles et al., 2004). For this reason, schools should be restructured if the full benefits of inclusion are to be achieved; that is, schools will need to consider cultural and symbolic changes to their structure to achieve genuine inclusion (Rizvi & Lingard, 1996). One example is ongoing professional development that compels teachers to examine critically issues such as (a) how student race shapes teacher expectations, (b) definitions of "acceptable behavior" underlying school and classroom discipline policies, (c) the cultural assumptions of parent involvement policies and programs, and (d) cultural assumptions about "proper" use of the English language as the medium used to assess student competence.

Distributive solutions fail to recognize the power relationships and structures of privilege that shape and sustain injustice (Christensen & Rizvi, 1996). Power and privilege shape tangible and intangible aspects of the educational system such as the goals of education, the curriculum, and the organizational structures and processes of schools. If the role of power and privilege is not examined explicitly, we run the risk of perpetuating longstanding inequalities suffered by members of other minority groups. In fact, it has been argued that racial minority students (particularly African Americans and Native Americans) may be experiencing this situation, as they have been overrepresented in traditional special education programs for decades (Artiles, 2003). Because *individualistic* models of social justice restrict analyses to the individual, racial minority students placed in special education end up adding to an already long list of imposed deficits and disadvantages (e.g., poor, linguistically delayed, distractible) an individually rooted disability label. Ironically, these special education practices are being carried out at a time when schools are striving to enhance access to and redistribute educational resources for students with disabilities. The cultural and historical forces (e.g., long-standing deficit views of minorities, meritocratic ideologies, White middle-class models of competence) that inform professionals' decisions to judge a racial minority student's performance as defiant, incompetent, or below average are invisible when analyses are based on individualistic models.

The meritocratic perspective has co-opted other forms of *individualistic* views of social justice (Christensen & Dorn, 1997). Inclusion discourses, particularly those justifying the need for inclusive education (i.e., rights and ethics and efficacy discourses), might be inadvertently lending support to this type of social justice. The idea of personal merit is perpetuated in an inclusive education model because individual deficits must be documented to receive special education services. By believing in the promises of the current accountability movement, inclusive education also is aligning with the idea of individual merit. The inclusion and accountability mandates stipulate that access to the general education curriculum (a distributive argument) will equalize educational opportunities for students with disabilities. As we know, the evidence of these policies' impact is measured on an individual basis through standardized testing. This way, the meritocratic assumption that school success and failure are individual endeavors is reiterated. From this vantage point, the school system and general education personnel contribute to perpetuating a meritocratic system because they deny responsibility for the production of students with disabilities' educational outcomes. This situation is reflected, for example, in current debates about the exclusion of special needs populations in testing requirements (Christensen & Dorn, 1997).

On the other hand, *communitarian* views of social justice, which shift attention away from individuals toward communities and society, have been criticized for providing only general statements and supporting the merit of its vision on a critique of *individualistic* models (Howe, 1996). This is problematic because a theory of social justice should provide specific guidelines and prescriptions for policy and practice; its value should not reside on a critique of other social justice models (Christensen & Dorn, 1997). Inclusion discourses tend to be critical of the traditional parallel system of special education. Across inclusion discourses (particularly the *implementation* discourse) there is a naïve assumption based on a *communitarian* premise that the transformation of current special education structures and the adoption of a new vocabulary about disability and programs will shape collective attitudes toward the formation of inclusive school communities. Unfortunately, there is a long history of failed educational reforms grounded in the same fallacious assumption. A theory of how educational systems change toward social justice models is missing in this literature (Christensen & Dorn, 1997).

A related limitation of the *communitarian* perspective is that "because the predominant community values that serve as the final arbiter on moral matters must meet no standards other than their own, communities are free to treat their members as they see fit" (Howe, 1996, p. 50). Let us remember that not long ago there was consensus in communities across the nation about racial segregation and school exclusion of children with disabilities. How is the *communitarian* model supposed to handle instances in which a community's consensus may not necessarily represent equitable or viable options for certain groups? In every community where there is consensus, there is dissent. How would dissenting minority needs be protected? What would happen to individuals or subgroups that do not abide by the core values and principles of the community? One could argue that current values and practices of the special education research community exemplify some of these risks. For instance, most research practices in special education are based on a culture-blind ideology as reflected in the lack of attention to racial and linguistic minority students in intervention research (Donovan & Cross, 2002). What are the long-term consequences of this situation for educational access and equal educational opportunity for racial and linguistic minority groups?

265

The Road Ahead

As a means to promote social justice for students with disabilities, the special education field is striving to consolidate inclusive education models. We argued that multiple discourses on inclusion coexist in these efforts and these discourses subscribe to disparate and often contradictory perspectives on social justice. *Individualistic* views of social justice have pervaded throughout the history of the field. Indeed, special education service delivery models were originally designed to assist individuals to compensate for characteristics (e.g., cognitive, behavioral) that put them at a disadvantage in schools (Howe, 1996). We also explained that the advent of market-driven perspectives is strengthening a version of *individualistic* social justice that further disadvantages certain communities in our society (e.g., racial and linguistic minorities) because historical oppression and exclusion legacies that still affect these groups are not taken into account to understand individual performance. A common criticism of *individualistic* approaches is that they leave intact the goals and structures of traditional education models that perpetuate inequalities (e.g., assessment procedures and discipline regulations based on the belief that achievement is the result of individual merit and White middle class assumptions about competence).

In contrast, *communitarian* philosophies strive to create learning communities in which relationships are based on care and responsibility. However, this paradigm is also fraught with challenges, including lack of specificity in its prescriptions and limitations of community-based forms of governance. Howe's compelling question addresses some of the risks associated with communitarian solutions: "wasn't depending on local communities the *modus operandi* before the litigation and legislation of the 1970s required local communities to do much more to educate children with disabilities?" (p. 60).

Little attention has been devoted to the potential consequences of this state of affairs for the *justification* and *implementation* of inclusive education models. What will be the future of inclusion discourses and how should the coexistence of multiple views of social justice be addressed? Should we strive to reduce the multiplicity of inclusion discourses and social justice strategies? Do some social justice perspectives offer fewer trade-offs for oppressed groups? Which social justice model can help us transcend the tensions special education has created between special treatment of students through intensive individualized interventions and access to educational opportunities in the general education system (Christensen, 1996; Minow, 1990)?

These questions do not have straight answers. Scholars have offered alternative perspectives that include relational paradigms (Christensen & Dorn, 1997) and models that integrate various approaches (e.g., liberal–egalitarian plus democratic equality of educational opportunity; Howe, 1996). For instance, Howe's proposed model calls for a participatory approach in which goals, tools (e.g., curricula), and practices are deliberated and negotiated through wide participation. More important, attention is given to the ideological and historical institutional assumptions about *difference* (Artiles, 1998).

We argue that for inclusion to live up to its promise of social justice, future work must craft and test transformative models that tackle individual as well as historical and structural forces because the "transformation of the social identity of one group [e.g., the dis-abled, the culturally different racial minority] will not occur if the social identity of the other group [e.g., the abled, the cultureless European American] remains intact" (Christensen, 1996, p. 76; see Figure 2). Transformative models are critically needed considering that a disproportionate number of students from oppressed groups (i.e., racial minorities) are placed in special education (Donovan & Cross, 2002). Scholarship that helps us understand the experiences of racial minority students as they negotiate multifaceted identities (disabled, racial minority) in inclusive programs that are committed to social justice is virtually nonexistent (Artiles, 2003).

Future inclusive education models based on a transformative view of social justice should avoid the contradictions created by economic-political (distributive view) or cultural (recognition or valo-

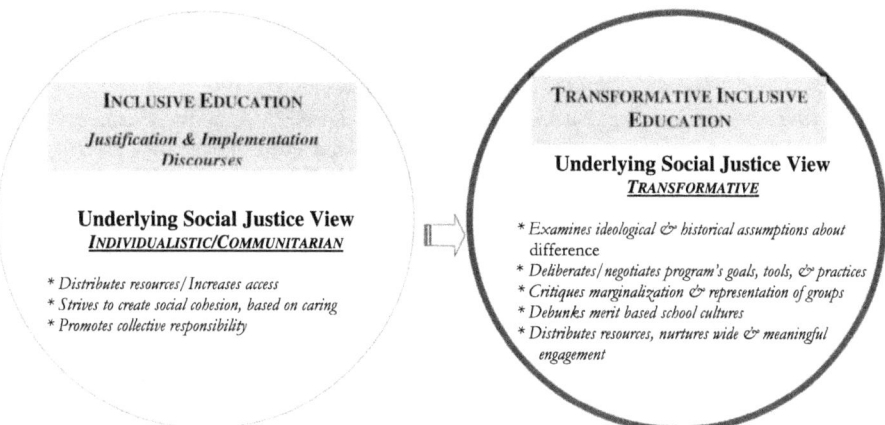

Figure 2. From a traditional social justice discourse in inclusive education to a transformative model of social justice.

rization) solutions (Christensen, 1996). The former aims to diffuse group differentiation by allocating resources that homogenize society's members (e.g., by equalizing access to jobs), whereas the latter reinforces social differentiation by recognizing a group's worth and needs (e.g., bilingual and special education policies; Minow, 1990). Future transformative models must embrace participatory strategies in which distribution of resources, access, and social cohesion constitutes the foundation of democratic egalitarian alternatives. In such models, deliberation and critical analyses are used to address individual and institutional forces (Howe, 1996). As Young suggested,

> Groups with different circumstances or forms of life should be able to participate together in public institutions without shedding their distinct identities or suffering disadvantage due to them. The goal is not to give special compensation to the deviant until they achieve normality, but rather to denormalize the way institutions formulate their rules by revealing the plural circumstances and needs that exist, or ought to exist, within them. (as cited in Howe, 1996, p. 55)

Acknowledgments

We are grateful to Stan Trent, Elizabeth Kozleski, and the journal editors for their feedback on earlier versions of this article. Writing of this article was supported by the National Center for Culturally Responsive Educational Systems under Grant No. H326E020003 awarded by the U. S. Department of Education's Office of Special Education Programs.

References

Ainscow, M. (1994). *Special needs in the classroom: A teacher education guide*. London: Unesco.

Artiles, A. (1998). The dilemma of difference: Enriching the disproportionality of discourse with theory and context. *The Journal of Special Education, 32*, 32–36.

Artiles, A. (2003). Special education's changing identity: Paradoxes and dilemmas in views of culture and space. *Harvard Educational Review, 78,* 164–202.

Artiles, A., Trent, S. C., & Palmer, J. (2004). Culturally diverse students in special education: Legacies and prospects. In J. A. Banks & C. M. Banks (Eds.), *Handbook of research on multicultural education* (2nd ed.; pp. 716–735). San Francisco: Jossey-Bass.

Christensen, C. (1996). Disabled, handicapped or disordered: "What's in a name?". In C. Christensen & F. Rizvi (Eds.), *Disability and the dilemmas of education and justice* (pp. 63–77). Buckingham, England: Open University Press.

Christensen, C., & Dorn, S. (1997). Competing notions of social justice and contradictions in special education reform. *The Journal of Special Education, 31,* 181–198.

Christensen, C., & Rizvi, F. (1996). *Disability and the dilemmas of education and justice.* Buckingham, England: Open University Press.

Donovan, S., & Cross, C. (Eds.). (2002). *Minority students in special and gifted education.* Washington, DC: National Academies Press.

Dyson, A. (1999). Inclusion and inclusions: Theories and discourses in inclusive education. In H. Daniels & P. Garner (Eds.), *World yearbook of education 1999: Inclusive education* (pp. 36–53). London: Kogan Page.

Howe, K. (1996). Educational ethics, social justice and children with disabilities. In C. Christensen & F. Rizvi (Eds.), *Disability and the dilemmas of education and justice* (pp. 46–62). Buckingham, England: Open University Press.

Johnson, J. (2004). Universal instruction design and critical (communication) pedagogy: Strategies for voice, inclusion, and social justice/change. *Equity and Excellence in Education, 37,* 145–153.

Lipsky, D., & Gartner, A. (1996). Equity requires inclusion: The future for all students with disabilities. In C. Christensen & F. Rizvi (Eds.), *Disability and the dilemmas of education and justice* (pp. 145–155). Buckingham, England: Open University Press.

Lipsky, D., & Gartner, A. (1998). Taking inclusion into the future. *Educational Leadership, 56,* 78–81.

Minow, M. (1990). *Making all the difference: Inclusion, exclusion, and American law.* Ithaca, NY: Cornell University Press.

Rawls, J. (1971). *A theory of justice.* Cambridge, MA: Belknap Press of Harvard University Press.

Rizvi, F., & Lingard, B. (1996). Disability, education and the discourses of justice. In C. Christensen & F. Rizvi (Eds.), *Disability and the dilemmas of education and justice* (pp. 9–26). Buckingham, England: Open University Press.

Skrtic, T. M. (1991). The special education paradox: Equity as the way to excellence. *Harvard Educational Review, 61,* 148–206.

Udvari-Solner, A. (1995). A process for adapting the curriculum in inclusive classrooms. In R. A. Villa & J. S. Thousand (Eds.), *Creating an inclusive school* (pp. 110–124). Alexandria, VA: Association for Supervision and Curriculum Development.

Varenne, H., & McDermott, R. (Eds.). (1999). *Successful failure: The school America builds.* Boulder, CO: Westview Press.

Vaughn, S., & Schumm, J. S. (1995). Responsible inclusion for students with learning disabilities. *Journal of Learning Disabilities, 28,* 264–270.

Young, I. M. (1990). Polity and group difference: A critique of the ideal of universal citizenship. In C. Sunstein (Ed.), *Feminism and political theory* (pp. 117–141). Chicago: University of Chicago Press.

James McLeskey
Nancy L. Waldron

Comprehensive School Reform and Inclusive Schools

In spite of the emphasis in public policy and the professional literature on developing inclusive programs for students with disabilities over the past 30 years, surprisingly little progress has been made in this regard in school districts across the United States. One approach to change that is currently being used with some success in general education and that has shown promise for developing more inclusive schools is comprehensive school reform (CSR). This article provides a brief description of an approach to CSR that has been used to develop programs that support a diverse range of students, including students with disabilities in general education classrooms. Preliminary research on this approach to school change suggests that CSR has the potential to provide teachers and administrators with a framework to develop successful, sustainable inclusive programs.

James McLeskey is a Professor in and Chair of the Department of Special Education at the University of Florida. Nancy L. Waldron is an Associate Professor in the Department of Educational Psychology at the University of Florida.

Correspondence should be addressed to James McLeskey, Department of Special Education, University of Florida, G315 Norman Hall, PO Box 117050, Gainesville, FL 32611. E-mail: mcleskey@coe.ufl.edu

However, further research is needed to document the effectiveness of CSR across settings and with a range of outcome measures.

MANY LEGISLATIVE INITIATIVES and federal regulations have been passed in recent decades (see Browder, Wakeman, & Flowers, this issue) to provide students with disabilities access to the general education curriculum and to require the same accountability standards as for students who do not have disabilities. In spite of these mandates, surprisingly little progress has been made nationally toward educating students with disabilities in general education classrooms (Danielson & Bellamy, 1989; McLeskey, Hoppey, Williamson, & Rentz, 2004; Williamson, McLeskey, Hoppey, & Rentz, 2006). Most of the change that has occurred in educating students with disabilities in general education classrooms at a national level has occurred in 10 to 15 states, whereas the remaining states have made very little progress (McLeskey & Henry, 1999; McLeskey et al., 2004; Williamson et al., 2006). Furthermore, much of the progress that appears to have been made on a national level results largely from increasing identification rates for students with the mildest disabilities, who continue to receive much of their education in general education classrooms after they are identified with a disability (McLeskey et al., 2004).

Much of this lack of progress has been attributed to the failure on the part of general and special educators to change general education classrooms and make them more accommodating for students with disabilities (Burstein, Sears, Wilcoxen, Cabello, & Spagna, 2004; McLeskey & Waldron, 2002b; Scruggs & Mastropieri, 1996). Burstein et al. state that currently available evidence suggests that "general education teachers feel unprepared to serve students with disabilities, have little time available to collaborate, and make few accommodations for students with special needs" (p. 104). Indeed, it is apparent that effecting and sustaining these changes has proven much more difficult than educators, researchers, or policy makers anticipated.

We would speculate that there are two major causes for this lack of progress in developing more inclusive programs. First, most mainstreaming and inclusive programs have been developed primarily by special educators as add on programs, without the substantive input of general educators (McLeskey & Waldron, 2000, 2002b). Research related to school change reveals that such programs result in superficial change, or what Goodman (1995, p. 1) has called "change without difference," which is infrequently sustained over time. In contrast, research on school change reveals that lasting, substantive change must transform current school practices, and cannot simply be an add-on (Fullan, 2001; McLeskey & Waldron, 2002b). More specifically, successful school change must alter not only organizational structures and policies related to individual schools, but also must alter the role and responsibilities of teachers, curriculum used in the classroom, methods for grouping students for instruction, attitudes and beliefs of teachers, and so forth. Such changes require teachers to reflect deeply on the changes that are made, and to incorporate these changes into their beliefs about schooling (Borko, 2004; Richardson & Placier, 2001) and their understanding about the culture of their school (Fullan, 2001; Sarason, 1982, 1990).

A second reason for the failure to successfully change schools is the perception on the part of many special educators that effective practices need to be identified and described for teachers, who will then proceed to implement the practices in classrooms (Boudah, Logan, & Greenwood, 2001; Carnine, 1997; Fuchs, Fuchs, Harris, & Roberts, 1996; Greenwood & Abbott, 2001). This *empirical–rational* approach to professional development (Chin & Benne, 1969) has proven to be largely ineffective, as the perspective that teachers are vessels into which knowledge is poured by an expert has resulted in little change in the practices of teachers (Borko, 2004; McLeskey & Waldron, 2002a; Richardson & Placier, 2001). In contrast to this approach, several researchers have noted the need to situate professional development within the context of a larger school change effort (Borko, 2004; McLeskey & Waldron, 2000, 2002a) that increases the likelihood that changes will occur in classroom practices that have a productive effect on student outcomes, and ensures that teachers and administrators will assume ownership of the changes that are made. This *normative–reeducative* approach (Chin and Benne, 1969) assumes that changes in teacher behavior result when professional development focuses "on providing autonomy for and cultivating growth in the people who make up the system and on increasing the problem solving capabilities of the system" (Richardson & Placier, 2001, p. 905).

Thus, research on school change and professional development has helped educators understand why add-on efforts at change have not worked, and have pointed the way toward the need for more comprehensive approaches to school change. More important, this research has provided new directions for developing effective, sustainable programs that improve educational outcomes for *all* students, and provide the necessary support so that general education classrooms may be changed to accommodate a broader range of student needs.

This article provides a description of one approach to comprehensive school reform (CSR) that has been used to develop programs that support a diverse range of students, including students with disabilities, in general education classrooms.

Before describing this approach to school change, a brief description of and definition for CSR in general education will be provided, as well as a brief discussion of the impact this movement has had on special education. This will be followed by a description of the approach used by McLeskey and Waldron (2000, 2002b) to develop what they have called inclusive school programs (ISPs). Finally, a brief review of research related to the effectiveness of the ISP model of school reform will be provided.

What Is CSR?

Over the past 2 decades, the two most important educational reform movements in general education have often been competing and contradictory (Borman, Hewes, Overman, & Brown, 2003). One of these approaches has emphasized top-down efforts to improve schools through changes in policies such as increased standards and regulations, increased core requirements, and lengthened school day and year (Desimone, 2004). In contrast to this top-down, policy-driven approach to educational reform, the second approach has emphasized local control over reforms, emphasizing approaches such as decentralized decision making and school-based management (Borman et al., 2003).

CSR efforts have been described as a third wave of educational reform, designed to reconcile these previous reform efforts. "The general spirit of today's reform efforts continues to articulate top-down standards, which dictate many of the changes in the content of schooling, but fundamentally leaves the process of school change up to the discretion of local educators" (Borman et al., 2003, p. 126). More specifically, CSR "focuses on improvement of entire schools rather than on particular populations of students within schools; and it is not limited to particular subjects, programs, or instructional methods" (Desimone, 2004, p. 433). Furthermore, it is assumed that special education in general and students with disabilities in particular will be a part of these reform efforts (Koh & Robertson, 2004), so that improvements in schools will have a positive effect on all students.

CSR and Special Education

The impact of the CSR movement on special education and students with disabilities has recently begun to be documented by researchers. In some instances, there is evidence that certain approaches to CSR explicitly target and attempt to address the needs of some students with disabilities (often those with mild disabilities) in inclusive settings (e.g., "Success for All " [Slavin & Madden, 2000a]; "Roots and Wings" [Slavin & Madden, 2000b]), whereas other models include statements of philosophy that are strongly aligned with inclusive practices (e.g., Coalition of Essential Schools [Sizer, 1992]). However, in spite of the emphasis on *all* students in many models of CSR, students with disabilities are often not part of reform efforts, and when special education is considered, inclusion is most often not a focus (Doyle & Owens, 2003; Koh & Robertson, 2004).

As a result of the lack of responsiveness of CSR models to students with disabilities, models of CSR have begun to emerge that have a primary focus on inclusion and making general education classrooms more accommodating for all students, including those with disabilities (Jorgenson, 1998; McLeskey & Waldron, 2000, 2002a; Peterson, 2000). The following section provides a brief description of one of these models that has been implemented in over 40 schools in several school districts.

One Approach to CSR With a Focus on Inclusion

McLeskey and Waldron (2000, 2002a) have worked collaboratively with teachers and administrators for the past 15 years to develop more effective programs that address a diverse range of student needs in general education classrooms. This work has resulted in the development of a systematic process for school change that has been successfully used in many schools. This approach to systematic school change is built on several principles that have guided the work (McLeskey

& Waldron, 2000, 2002a, 2002b). These principles include the following.

1. *To be successful, change must have the support of central office administrators, the building principal, and teachers.* This suggests that top-down and bottom-up support are necessary, and addresses the contradictory nature of previous reform efforts. Furthermore, this principle suggests that the active support of the local school principal and a large proportion of teachers is needed before any attempt at CSR begins.

2. *Schools must be empowered to manage their own change.* Although educators from outside the local school may provide accountability measures, local schools are given the responsibility to determine how their school will change to meet these standards. This assures that changes will be built on the perceived strengths of the local school, and that local school personnel will own and thus support these changes.

3. *School change efforts that address inclusion must address improving a school for all students, and not just for students with disabilities.* If students with disabilities are to be an integral part of the academic and social community of the local school (McLeskey & Waldron, 2000), changes to provide support for these students cannot be made in isolation. Moreover, if such an add-on approach to change is used, students with disabilities become even more marginalized in the school, these changes are not integrated into the overall culture of the school, and most often the changes are not sustained. Simply put, any substantive change that is made in a school influences all students, thus it is not possible to address the needs of students with disabilities in isolation. Using a comprehensive approach to school reform also recognizes the pragmatic perspective of the classroom teacher, who is not interested in addressing only the needs of students with disabilities (or any single group of students, for that matter, however defined) but has much more interest in approaches that help him or her address the needs of *all* students in his or her class.

4. *Change must be tailored to the particular needs of students and the expertise of educators within each school.* There is no fixed model to guide change. Change in special education has long been viewed as the identification of a model or evidence-based practice that is presented to teachers and then used in the classroom. Ample evidence indicates that this approach to change does not work (Fuchs et al., 1996; Fullan, 2001; Gersten, Chard, & Baker, 2000), as it fails to recognize the complexity of schools and the power of local teachers and administrators to influence substantive changes in their schools (Goodman, 1995; McLeskey & Waldron, 2002a). Moreover, any model or approach to change must be subject to the needs and strengths of the local school, and will thus be adapted as it is implemented in a given setting.

5. *Changes must be built on proven effective practices.* Research conducted over the past several decades has provided much information regarding effective instructional practices (e.g., see Bond & Castagnera, this issue). Many of these practices are designed to improve academic outcomes for students who struggle to learn in general education classrooms, and are thus beneficial for students with disabilities and others who lack the skills to be successful in general education classrooms.

6. *Changes should focus on making differences ordinary throughout all school settings for all students.* The development of genuine, inclusive classrooms that accommodate the needs of all students should result in classrooms in which "wide-ranging differences are accommodated as a natural part of the classroom day" (McLeskey & Waldron, 2002b, p. 68). To make classrooms more accommodating, resources may be added to the classroom (e.g., coteaching or adding a paraeducator), or alterations may be made in classroom curriculum, instruction, or organization (e.g., class-wide peer tutoring, cooper-

ative learning). In these classrooms, what counts as special may not stand out. As Pugach (1995) has noted, "One measure might be the degree to which observers cannot tell, and do not need to be interested in, which students were formerly labeled as having a disability" (p. 220).

Thus, general education classes are transformed, and become settings in which a broad range of differences are an ordinary part of the school day.

Ten Steps Toward Developing an ISP

With the six guiding principles in mind, we work with schools using a systematic approach to change. It is important to note that although we suggest that schools use the following 10-step approach to achieve this change, we encourage teachers and local administrators to adapt this approach to the particular needs of their local school (see principle 4, p. 272). For a more detailed description of the 10-step approach to school change, see McLeskey and Waldron (2000).

Begin With a Discussion of Schooling for All Students

At the beginning of the change process, we encourage teachers and administrators in local schools to have an open and full discussion of schooling for all students. The ultimate purposes of this discussion are to ensure support for beginning the change process, to determine specific areas (e.g., more accommodating general education classrooms, better behavior throughout the school, improved reading achievement) that should be the focus of initial change efforts, and to begin the development of a shared vision for the successful education of all students. This discussion ensures that all teachers understand and appreciate the fact that all students are important (including students with the full range of disabilities), and that change to accommodate and better support all students requires major changes in their school. We encourage teachers and administrators at this point to develop a brief vision statement that will guide their deliberations. For example, "The goal of this school change activity is to prepare and support teachers to better meet the needs of all students who enter their classrooms." This discussion should continue throughout the change process, and should serve to facilitate several of the steps that follow, as the plan for CSR is developed and implemented.

Form a Team

Ideally, every teacher and administrator in a school should be involved in each decision as a CSR effort moves forward. However, time constraints make this impossible. The best alternative we have identified is to have a group of well respected teachers and administrators who are representative of the many perspectives that exist within the school to form a core planning team to guide the change effort. Initially, the team should develop knowledge and skills regarding the change process, as well as skills in group process and management. This planning team will provide leadership as the change process progresses.

Examine Your School

One of the first activities of the planning team should be to examine their own school. We have found that it is rare that any teacher or administrator fully understands all of the issues that face a school across grade levels and subject areas. This process can ensure that the critical issues that exist within the school are brought to the attention to the planning team and addressed by this group. Examining the local school will also serve to ensure that as changes occur, the planning team will be sensitive to existing workloads. It will provide information regarding available resources and how they might be used more efficiently and effectively, and will provide stakeholders with the necessary information to develop a plan that is tailored to the needs and preferences of the entire school community. We have developed a comprehensive activity that we recommend planning teams use in carrying out this process (McLeskey & Waldron, 2000).

Examine Other Schools

We have found that one of the most powerful influences on school change is having staff from a reforming school visit, observe, and interact with staff from a school that has successfully completed CSR. These visits provide teachers and administrators the opportunity to explore the "nuts and bolts" of change with educators who have been through the process, as well as to observe how other schools have implemented such change. This gives teachers a mental picture of the result of such a school change effort, and helps them to realize that such change is possible. School visits also serve to give planning team members ideas about possible changes that may work in their school, as well as changes that they want to avoid.

Develop a Plan

After the first four steps, school planning teams are ready to gather together the information they have collected and develop a plan for change in their school. This plan should be comprehensive and detailed, and should address how school organization, curriculum and instruction, teacher roles and responsibilities, and so forth will be changed to better meet the needs of all students. Furthermore, this plan should include documented effective practices and address the need to provide professional development and related support to teachers so that they have the necessary knowledge, skills, and dispositions to teach successfully as school change occurs.

Review and Discuss the Plan With the School Community

One of the realizations that occurs to many planning team members once they have developed a plan for CSR is that they become outsiders, and have to work to bring other members of the school community up to speed regarding the proposed changes. To ensure the ownership of the plan for change by the entire school community, it is important that the plan be a working document, and that the entire school community have input into the final plan. This ensures that all voices are heard, and maximizes the extent to which members of the school community feel ownership for the plan.

Incorporate Changes Into the Plan

The length of stages 6 and 7 will vary, depending on the extent to which the entire school community has been kept up to date regarding the work of the planning team as the plan for CSR is developed, and the extent to which the school community finds the plan acceptable. There are two important factors to consider at this stage. First, there will always be concern and disagreement with any plan for CSR. The planning team and school principal must make a judgment regarding when to move ahead with the plan, even through support is not unanimous. Some schools vote on a final plan, and only move forward if a certain proportion (one half, two thirds, or three fourths) of the faculty support the plan. Another important factor to consider is that the plan will never address all issues or be perfect, and should continue to be subject to change, even (perhaps especially) after implementation (for more on this, see step 10). Fullan (2001) suggests that a *ready, fire, aim* approach to change is a reasonable approach at this stage, to ensure that school planning teams do not spend too much time planning, in an attempt to develop a perfect plan. In short, planning teams should carefully develop a plan and take into account everything that seems important but anticipate that once the plan is implemented new issues will arise that will require changes in the plan.

Get Ready

Many schools have developed their plans for change during the fall and winter semesters of one year, and implemented the plans in the fall of the following year. This provides time during the spring and summer for professional development and additional planning as teachers and administrators get ready for the changes that will occur.

Possible topics for professional development may include teaming and coteaching, classroom accommodation for diverse student needs, curricular adaptations, behavior management strategies, and so forth. Furthermore, teachers will need planning time to work with colleagues to discuss and plan the curriculum and instructional changes that are to occur.

Implement the Plan

As we noted previously, schools typically implement the plan they have developed during the fall of the school year, after careful planning through several months during the previous school year. It is important that teachers who are collaborating to support the newly implemented plan have common planning time to address issues that arise as the plan is implemented.

Monitor, Evaluate, and Change the Plan, as Needed

Finally, teachers and administrators must ensure that ongoing time is available for the planning teams as well as for teachers who are intimately involved in implementation so that the plan may be monitored, evaluated, and changed, as needed. This ensures the effectiveness of the ISP in improving student outcomes, and provides data on needed changes in the program.

Outcomes of CSR Using the ISP Model

Approximately a third of the 40 elementary, middle, and high schools with whom we have worked have made substantive changes in their overall school as they have developed and implemented CSR plans. Another third of the schools have made more modest changes (e.g., changes at two grade levels or across two teams in a middle school). The final third of the schools have made very few changes, and we would characterize the ISP model as largely ineffective for those schools (McLeskey & Waldron, 2002b). This finding is not unusual (Fullan, 2001; Gersten, Vaughn, Deshler, & Schiller, 1997), as previous research suggests that comprehensive school efforts are met with different levels of success across schools (Borman et al., 2003).

Our research with respect to the ISP schools indicates that student outcomes are at least as good, and often better when students are in inclusive programs, when compared to separate class special education programs. For example, we compared the achievement of students with learning disabilities in three ISP elementary schools with students in three schools that used traditional, pull-out special education programs (Waldron & McLeskey, 1998). We found that students with milder learning disabilities made more progress in reading in the ISP schools, whereas students with more severe learning disabilities made comparable academic progress across the two settings.

A further study investigated teachers' perspectives on the educational progress students with disabilities made in ISP schools (Waldron, McLeskey, & Pacchiano, 1999). Teachers in six ISP elementary schools were interviewed regarding a range of issues. The teachers "strongly supported the perspective that students with disabilities made significant gains related to their academic achievement skills during the school year, with most students surpassing the expectations of their general and special education teachers" (p. 145). These teachers felt that increased expectations and exposure to a broader range of curriculum had a positive influence on the students' achievement and placed more emphasis on factors other than academic test scores when describing the effects of the ISP. Furthermore, the teachers noted that although changes in students' behavior might not translate directly into improved test scores, specific behaviors such as better general organizational skills, improved study skills, and a greater willingness to take risks, were important for the long-term success of the students. Teachers in the ISPs believed that students without disabilities benefited academically and socially from placement in these programs (McLeskey, Waldron, So, Swanson, & Loveland, 2001; Waldron et al., 1999). Other investigations have also revealed that students without disabilities, especially low-achieving students, often benefit academically from placement in a well designed inclusive program (e.g., see Janney & Snell, this issue).

Teachers also addressed the social behavior of students in the ISP schools, along with the relationships they had with other students. The teachers had no general concerns about increased behavior problems, with several noting that the behavior of many of the students with disabilities had improved. They believed that the students were influenced by positive models of appropriate behavior in general education classrooms, as well as the desire to fit in. A small number of students did present significant issues for teachers due to their aggressive, disruptive behaviors. Some of the teachers were able to make adaptations in their classrooms to address these issues, whereas in other instances students were removed from general education classrooms, a typical scenario for all of the ISPs where we have worked. Although the vast majority of students can be successfully included, some students present such difficult challenges that teachers and support personnel cannot design a program to successfully meet their needs.

Teachers also stated that students with disabilities were fitting in better in their classes than many of the teachers had anticipated they would, although it did not occur immediately or automatically. Teachers took an active role in helping students build friendships with other students with disabilities, as well as students without disabilities. Several teachers noted that "the social skills and friendships which students with disabilities were developing in the general education classroom were critical preparation for life, and were the most positive outcome of the ISP" (Waldron et al., 1999, p. 149).

Finally, we have conducted research on teachers' support for the ISPs that were developed in their schools (McLeskey et al., 2001; Waldron et al., 1999). These investigations were designed to study teachers' perspectives on well developed inclusive programs, and did not attempt to address general teacher attitudes toward inclusion, or attitudes toward less successful programs. For more information, see Scruggs and Mastropieri, 1996. The investigations revealed that teachers were strongly supportive of the inclusive programs in their schools. For example, we surveyed teachers in three ISP schools, and compared their responses to teachers in three schools with traditional special education programs. The teachers in the ISP schools were significantly more positive regarding inclusive programs than the teachers from the traditional schools. Teachers in the ISP schools had significantly more positive perspectives regarding how well prepared they were to teach in an inclusive classroom, and had significantly fewer concerns about their possible roles and functions in the inclusive program. In addition, teachers in the ISP schools had significantly more positive perspectives on how the ISP would influence student outcomes. Interviews with teachers in six ISP schools provided further support for these findings (Waldron et al., 1999). These teachers had strong, positive perspectives on the impact the ISP had on student academic outcomes and behavior.

Conclusion

Preliminary research on one approach to CSR that focuses on making general education classrooms more accommodating for all students (McLeskey & Waldron, 2000, 2002b), including those with disabilities, suggests that this approach has the potential to provide teachers and administrators with a framework to develop successful, sustainable inclusive programs. However, more research is needed to further document the effectiveness of this and other approaches to CSR, as very limited research is available at present. In particular, additional research is needed to document the effectiveness of different approaches to CSR, as well as the effectiveness of these approaches to school change across settings (e.g., urban/rural/suburban, elementary/secondary), and using a range of outcome measures (e.g., content area measures in secondary schools, measures of social–behavioral outcomes).

The lack of progress that has been made in the past 30 years toward educating students with disabilities in less restrictive settings strongly suggests that new approaches to developing inclusive programs are needed. Although CSR is a time-intensive, school-by-school approach to change, it offers much promise as a framework that may be used by principals and teachers to develop successful, sustainable inclusive programs. Preliminary evidence suggests that these programs have the potential to improve educational outcomes for all students, especially those who make less than desired academic progress and struggle to meet current accountability goals.

References

Borko, H. (2004). Professional development and teacher learning: Mapping the terrain. *Educational Researcher, 33*(8), 3–15.

Borman, G., Hewes, G., Overman, L., & Brown, S. (2003). Comprehensive school reform and achievement: A meta-analysis. *Review of Educational Research, 73*, 125–230.

Boudah, D., Logan, K., & Greenwood, C. (2001). The research to practice projects: Lessons learned about changing teacher practice. *Teacher Education and Special Education, 24*, 290–303.

Burstein, N., Sears, S., Wilcoxen, A., Cabello, B., & Spagna, M. (2004). Moving toward inclusive practices. *Remedial and Special Education, 25*, 104–116.

Carnine, D. (1997). Bridging the research-to-practice gap. *Exceptional Children, 63*, 513–521.

Chin, R., & Benne, K. (1969). General strategies for effecting changes in human systems. In W. Bennis, K. Benne, & R. Chin (Eds.), *The planning of change* (2nd ed., pp. 32–59). New York: Holt, Rinehart, & Winston.

Danielson, L., & Bellamy, T. (1989). State variation in placement of children with handicaps in segregated environments. *Exceptional Children, 55*, 448–455.

Desimone, L. (2004). How can comprehensive school reform models be successfully implemented? *Review of Educational Research, 72*, 433–479.

Doyle, M., & Owens, L. (2003). How-to high: Analyses and processes in Chicago high schools. In D. Fisher & N. Frey (Eds.), *Inclusive urban schools* (pp. 151–174). Baltimore: Brookes.

Fuchs, D., Fuchs, L., Harris, A., & Roberts, P. H. (1996). Bridging the research-to-practice gap with mainstreaming assistance teams: A cautionary tale. *School Psychology Quarterly, 11*, 244–266.

Fullan, M. (2001). *The new meaning of educational change* (3rd ed.), New York: Teachers College Press.

Gersten, R., Chard, D., & Baker, S. (2000). Factors enhancing sustained use of research-based instructional practices. *Journal of Learning Disabilities, 33*, 445–457.

Gersten, R., Vaughn, S., Deshler, D., & Schiller, E. (1997). What we know about using research findings: Implications for improving special education practice. *Journal of Learning Disabilities, 30*, 466–476.

Goodman, J. (1995). Change without difference: School restructuring in historical perspective. *Harvard Educational Review, 65*(1), 1–29.

Greenwood, C., & Abbott, M. (2001). The research to practice gap in special education. *Teacher Education and Special Education, 24*, 276–289.

Jorgenson, C. (1998). *Restructuring high schools for all students*. Baltimore: Brookes.

Koh, M., & Robertson, J. (2004). School reform models and special education. *Education and Urban Society, 35*, 421–442.

McLeskey, J., & Henry, D. (1999). Inclusion: What progress is being made across states? *Teaching Exceptional Children, 31*(5), 56–62.

McLeskey, J., Hoppey, D., Williamson, P., & Rentz, T. (2004). Is inclusion an illusion? An examination of national and state trends toward the education of students with learning disabilities in general education classrooms. *Learning Disabilities: Research & Practice, 19*, 109–115.

McLeskey, J., & Waldron, N. (2000). *Inclusive education in action: Making differences ordinary*. Alexandria, VA: Association for Supervision and Curriculum Development.

McLeskey, J., & Waldron, N. (2002a). Professional development and inclusive schools: Reflections on effective practice. *Teacher Educator, 37*, 159–172.

McLeskey, J., & Waldron, N. (2002b). School change and inclusive schools: Lessons learned from practice. *Phi Delta Kappan, 84*(1), 65–72.

McLeskey, J., Waldron, N., So, T. H., Swanson, K., & Loveland, T. (2001). Perspectives of teachers toward inclusive school programs. *Teacher Education and Special Education, 24*, 108–115.

Peterson, M. (2000). *Key elements of whole schooling*. Detroit, MI: Wayne State University, Renaissance Community Press.

Pugach, M. (1995). On the future of imagination in inclusive schooling. *The Journal of Special Education, 29*, 212–223.

Richardson, V., & Placier, P. (2001). Teacher change. In V. Richardson (Ed.), *Handbook of research on teacher education* (4th ed.; pp. 905–947). Washington, DC: American Educational Research Association.

Sarason, S. B. (1982). *The culture of the school and the problem of change* (2nd ed.). Boston: Allyn & Bacon.

Sarason, S. B. (1990). *The predictable failure of educational reform.* San Francisco: Jossey-Bass.

Scruggs, T., & Mastropieri, M. (1996). Teacher perceptions of mainstreaming/inclusion, 1958–1995: A research synthesis. *Exceptional Children, 63,* 59–74.

Sizer, T. (1992). *Horace's school: Redesigning the American high school.* New York: Houghton Mifflin.

Slavin, R., & Madden, N. (2000a). Research on achievement outcomes of Success for All: A summary and response to critics. *Phi Delta Kappan, 82,* 38–40, 59–66.

Slavin, R., & Madden, N. (2000b). *Roots and wings: Effects of whole-school reform on student achievement* (Report 36). Baltimore: Johns Hopkins University, Center for Research on the Education of Students Placed At Risk. (ERIC Document Reproduction Series No. ED432804).

Waldron, N., & McLeskey, J. (1998). The impact of a full-time inclusive school program (ISP) on the academic achievement of students with mild and severe learning disabilities. *Exceptional Children, 64,* 395–405.

Waldron, N., McLeskey, J., & Pacchiano, D. (1999). Giving teachers a voice: Teachers' perspectives regarding elementary inclusive school programs (ISPs). *Teacher Education and Special Education, 22,* 141–153.

Williamson, P., McLeskey, J., Hoppey, D., & Rentz, T. (2006). Educating students with mental retardation in general education classrooms: An analysis of national and state trends. *Exceptional Children, 72,* 347–361.

Virginia Roach
Christine Salisbury

Promoting Systemic, Statewide Inclusion From the Bottom Up

Educators have been challenged to meet the needs of students with disabilities in the least restrictive environment. Although this mandate has existed for 30 years, local educators report difficulties with program planning; graduation and grading of students with disabilities; recruitment and retention of qualified teachers; ensuring access of all students to the general education curriculum; training in collaborative planning and teaching; and placing students in the least restrictive setting. These challenges inhibit educators' ability to include students with disabilities in general education and are largely the by-product of district and state policy. This article describes a bottom-up, context-specific change model that focused on providing professional development at each level (local to state) of the system and fostering communication across the levels. This strategy produced lasting change in 2 states in policy and local implementation of policy and serves as a model for teachers and principals seeking to promote inclusion.

Virginia Roach is Assistant Professor of Educational Administration at The George Washington University. Christine Salisbury is the Director of the Child and Family Development Center at the University of Illinois-Chicago.

Correspondence should be addressed to Virginia Roach, Educational Administration, 2134 G Street, N.W., The George Washington University, Washington, D.C. 20052. E-mail: vroach@gwu.edu

IN THE 30 YEARS since the original passage of the federal special education law (Education for All Handicapped Children Act of 1975), teachers and building-level administrators have increasingly supported the needs of students with disabilities in the least restrictive environment. Over the past 10 to 15 years, progressively more general and special educators have collaborated to assist students with disabilities in the general education classroom as part of *inclusion* (National Association of State Boards of Education, 1992) and changes to federal law (Individuals With Disabilities Education Improvement Act [IDEIA] of 2004). Yet, even as teachers and principals employ new instructional and staffing strategies in schools, they have reported district- and state-level challenges with respect to inclusion and program planning; graduation and grading of students with disabilities; recruitment and retention of qualified teachers; ensuring access of all students to the general education curriculum; training in collaborative planning and teaching; and placing students in the least restrictive setting. These challenges inhibit teachers' and principals' ability to include students with disabilities in the general education program (Bowen & Klass, 1993; Buswell, Schaffner, & Seyler, 1999; Fisher & Frey, 2001; Villa & Thousand, 2000).

The challenges cited are often beyond the control of a single teacher or principal. The issues are dictated by state and local policy, and significantly impact how schools operate and how children perform. Throughout the 1990s, educators increasingly identified policy areas that needed to be addressed to align the intent of the IDEIA with actual school-level practice (McDonnell & McLaughlin, 1997; McLaughlin, Henderson, & Rhim, 1998; Salisbury, Strieker, Roach, & McGregor, 2001). Understanding the relationship between policy and practice can help local educators negotiate the system to support students with disabilities and their families. Employing change strategies that loop between policy and practice can create continuous feedback to policymakers and educators to ensure that goals, policy, and practice are mutually supporting.

In 1995, the Consortium for Inclusive Schooling Practices (CISP) was created with federal funding to help fill the gap between the intent of federal law and the implementation of policy and practices at the state and local level. Over a 7-year period, CISP employed a three-pronged strategy in four states that focused on: (a) providing professional development and assistance concurrently at several levels of the service delivery system; (b) incorporating a unique set of stakeholders in the process of developing greater expertise and knowledge among the people in the system; and (c) integrating the levels of the system, such as classroom, building, district, and state, through feedback forums to promote communication and problem solving within and across levels in the system. This article describes the change model employed by CISP, how the model was successfully implemented in two states, and recommendations for those who wish to try this change strategy.

CISP adopted a bottom-up, context-specific, change strategy for their work (Chin & Benne, 1985). Rather than assuming that a traditional top-down transfer of knowledge will change behavior, the bottom-up approach assumes that change occurs as participants change their orientation to old behaviors and develop commitments to new ones. Chin and Benne argued that "change in attitudes, values, skills, and significant relationships, not just changes in knowledge, information, or intellectual rationales for action and practice" (p. 23) are necessary for promoting changes in patterns of practice. We used this theory because it has been linked to sustained change among adults (Dirkx, Blodgett, & Turner, n.d.; Kronley & Handley, 2001; Marks & Wright, 2002; Sargent, 2000). The bottom-up change model takes into consideration the specific context in which the change must occur and presumes that changes in attitudes, values, and skills precede changes in practice (Chin & Benne, 1985). Furthermore, because the top-down change strategy had been applied through federal law since 1976 with limited success, we reasoned that a bottom-up approach encompassing significant stakeholders and powerbrokers at the building, district, and state level, would be more effective (Bodilly, 1998; Deal, 1990; Gersten & Brengelman, 1996).

Elements of the Change Model

We constructed a change model based on a bottom-up theory that was grounded in state–local contexts and specific interventions based on building-level knowledge, skills, and problem-focused communication, as well as linked to changes at the policy and practice level (see Figure 1).

Contextual Factors

When we began development of our model for change, we needed to account for a variety of contextual forces. First, both amendments to IDEIA and case law clarified the presumption that students with disabilities would be included in the general education program and receive a free appropriate public education in the least restrictive environment in their neighborhood schools (Sands, Kozelski, & French, 2000; Skrtic, 1991).

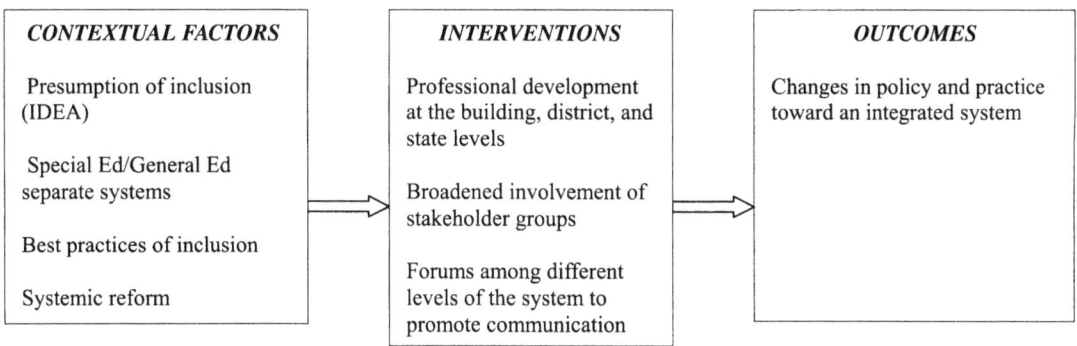

Figure 1. CISP Change Model.

Second, despite this presumption in federal law, special and general education systems across the United States were largely separate and distinct (Moscovitch, 1993; National Association of State Boards of Education, 1992). Third, there was an established and growing body of effective approaches for supporting students with disabilities, in general education programs and classrooms (McGregor & Vogelsberg, 1998; Villa & Thousand, 1995; Wang, Reynolds, & Walberg, 1988). Finally, school reform was increasingly approached from a systemic perspective, instead of approaching one student, or one problem, at a time (Fuhrman, 1993; Fullan, 1993; Fullan & Miles, 1992; Smith & O'Day, 1991). The systemic approach acknowledges "the interdependence among the various systems and parts of systems that provide services and support to children and youth" (Salisbury et al., 2001, p. 3). We designed our change approach in ways that would assist states and local districts in uniting their separate special and general education systems to support the inclusion of students with disabilities in the general education program.

Interventions

Our change model involved three interventions: (a) providing professional development at the building, district, and state levels through training and technical assistance; (b) incorporating a unique set of stakeholders in the professional development process; and (c) promoting communication and problem solving through feedback forums within and across levels of the system to resolve differences in what policies intended and their implementation in practice.

Professional development. We employed knowledge and skill-building activities at the building, district, and state level as one element of intervention. At the building level, project staff evaluated the inclusiveness of each school's practices using observations and a school climate survey. Guided by those assessments, CISP staff developed an action plan with each school based on the priorities identified by school personnel. CISP staff provided technical assistance to teachers and building principals to help them identify beliefs, attitudes, expectations, structures, and practices that functioned as barriers to the inclusion of all students in general education classrooms. CISP then helped the educators in the building learn strategies for addressing those barriers (e.g., changing team teaching practices, modifying school schedules, differentiating instruction, and developing individual educational plans that were grounded in the general education curriculum). At the high school level, special education faculty were reassigned to discipline-specific departments such as English and science, rather than isolated in their own special education department. In addition, technical assistance was provided using a *feeder path* approach. That is, CISP directed its training–technical assistance efforts toward teachers and principals across elementary schools that fed into middle schools, which in turn fed into the high school. This strategy allowed the district to transition students from one inclusive school to another and in the process, enhanced the system-wide effects of the work.

At the district level, project staff focused on issues generated at the school level, as well as on concerns generated by district-level personnel. Project staff provided information related to aligning the academic program with special educational supports such as adaptive technology, physical therapy, and school-wide behavior management programs. Project staff helped school personnel discuss integration among the different levels of schools: elementary, middle, and high school. Based on the identified needs of the district and school, discussions were facilitated about program and policy. For example, district personnel engaged in discussions about models for deploying specialized support personnel (e.g., occupational and speech therapists) regionally and in a consultative fashion, rather than always as direct service providers. Principals were provided information on the success of inclusive schooling models as measured by student achievement and cost data. Project staff presented information and updates on our work to local school board members, who are often left out of the loop in such program delivery discussions until a problem surfaces in the community. Special education directors at the local level were provided information that clarified state regulations and staffing requirements, as well as service delivery options, that the special education directors thought were prohibited by state or federal law.

In each state, a policy study was conducted to determine the level of integration between the special and general education systems. Assistance at the state level included providing analysis of the state's special education funding formula and securing technical assistance from other national experts for the state agency personnel to develop legislative proposals for change. State technical assistance also included identifying areas of state regulation that needed to be changed based on working with the local districts and schools. CISP staff served as a convener at the state level to bring legislative, budget, and education agency staff together to discuss issues associated with inclusion and potential regulatory, budgeting, and policy changes.

Unique set of stakeholders. Throughout this process, one of the core principles of our approach was to "be intentional about broadening representation at the table" (Salisbury et al., 2001, p. 7). One of the key targets of this work was to break down the barriers between general and special education to promote inclusive policies, structures, and practices. CISP was consistent in defining inclusion as "a philosophy that undergirds the *entire* educational system" (p. 3, italics added). Using the core principles of inclusion and representation, stakeholders were recruited based on their positions within the general education system. We did not want to be labeled as just another special education project. To counteract the phenomenon of rounding up the usual players, CISP staff recruited department of education and legislative staff from outside special education as the primary target audience.

Another unique feature of this change strategy was the direct involvement of the state board of education in the change process. State boards of education are the policymaking body at the state level that governs pre-K–12 education in most states. State boards set the vision for education in the state, establish budget priorities, enact rules and regulations, and conduct program evaluations. In many states, decisions of the state board of education carry the force of law. Despite the potential influence of this governing body, they are often overlooked in education change models.

At the district level, mirroring the state-level activity, project staff explicitly sought the participation and direction from the local board of education, another often overlooked governing body whose impact can be significant. Although local boards of education are not particularly known to lead inclusive initiatives, they are known for squelching such initiatives when they have not been fully included in the process from the beginning (Roach, Ashcroft, & Stamp, 1995). CISP sought input from the local board members in each district at the inception of the change process and at regular intervals thereafter.

At the district and building levels, as with the state level, the primary focus was on recruiting general educators and building administrators to the effort. Participants also included special education personnel. In some instances, this project was the first time the special and general education personnel had worked together. The stakeholders recruited for this work were integral to the communication and feedback process used to support systemic change.

Forums among different levels of the system and problem-based communication. Consistent with a bottom-up, context-specific theory of change, CISP created a number of forums for stakeholders at all levels of the system to provide feedback to participants at other levels of the system. These forums created a dynamic change process that illuminated barriers within the system and provided an opportunity to directly address misconceptions among stakeholders at each level. Indeed, the promise of direct communication with other levels of the system through these feedback forums was an incentive to many participants to engage, and remain, in the process. The forums were designed as structured, interactive meetings of stakeholders within and across systems and were used to identify issues, barriers, and potential solutions. The feedback loop process was characterized by the following elements:

- *Context-specific outcome orientation.* Each feedback activity was focused on achieving a state or district priority.
- *Continuous feedback loop.* Policy approaches were proposed to families, teachers, and principals, and their feedback contributed to further deliberations among policymakers, educators, and families.
- *Participatory.* In each state and district in which CISP worked, all stakeholders were actively involved in developing the objectives, design, and implementation of the project and technical assistance.
- *Explicit, rather than informal.* Many states and districts employ an informal feedback loop to get input on policy needs and recommended changes from teachers and principals. In other instances, policymakers rely on the grapevine and anecdotes to learn about local-level policy implementation issues. In contrast, the purpose of the CISP forums was explicitly to provide feedback within and across levels of the system.

The forums provided opportunities for communication and feedback among stakeholders who often did not know each other prior to this project.

Outcomes

CISP worked in three districts within each of four states and amassed considerable information about the promotion of inclusive policies and practices at the state, district, and school levels. Following are two examples of how the change process was applied. In State A, new policy resulted from our work. In State B, policy was clarified and the implementation of inclusive practices was expanded at the local level.

State A

In 1995, the State Board of Education identified funding as a key policy area affecting the delivery of inclusive services and supports. Special education funding in State A was widely recognized as problematic when CISP started work in the state. In 1994, prior to CISP's involvement in the state, the legislature asked the Legislative Analyst's Office, the Department of Education, and the Department of Finance to design a new funding formula for special education. A proposal was introduced by a state senator in the legislature in 1995 but was defeated, chiefly because larger school districts in the state were benefiting from the existing inequitable distribution of special education funds.

CISP worked with legislative staff to reignite their willingness to try to address the funding issue. Simultaneously, CISP staff began to work with a coalition of the largest school districts in the state (those who had blocked the earlier legislation) to determine what provisions would need to be present in a new formula for the large districts to sign on. As a result of this activity and informal prodding from legislative staff, a permanent, state-level, independent policy commission took up the issue of special education funding reform. CISP provided consultation, as well as written input, and facilitated the involvement of nationally known special education finance researchers in the work of the commission. CISP staff worked with the lobbyists from the large districts and a member of the state legislature who agreed to sponsor legislation. In addition, CISP staff facilitated informational sessions for district administrators across the state to gather support for the proposed change in the funding model. The outcome of these efforts and others produced a new special education funding bill. This bill was passed in the legislature and signed into law in 1997.

State B

At the beginning of the project, CISP staff conducted a study of education policies in State B and met with the State Board of Education to determine the members' thoughts regarding inclusion. CISP recommended that the Board increase its communication with stakeholders because the Board perceived that there was no outcry for inclusive education in the state, despite the fact that a major class-action lawsuit had recently been settled on that very point. The Board determined that CISP could provide support by conducting forums to determine sentiment toward inclusion and what stakeholders felt was needed to further support inclusion in the state.

CISP and the State Department of Education jointly sponsored focus groups at six regional forums throughout the state. A variety of stakeholders were represented at each forum, including families, teachers, building principals, district special education directors and superintendents, teacher educators, local school board members, and members of the State Board of Education. The primary objective was to obtain public perceptions about inclusive schooling practices for students with and without disabilities, as well as to obtain stakeholder input on how to increase and improve inclusive education in the state. Of the many issues explored, two major recommendations emerged: (a) adopt a state philosophy or vision statement on inclusive education; and (b) review state policies and regulations in personnel training and funding.

In response to the previous recommendations, the State Department of Education developed a booklet about inclusive education practices. The purpose of the booklet was to clarify the state's policy regarding special education in the least restrictive environment and to answer commonly asked questions about inclusive schooling practices. The booklet was distributed widely throughout the state and was one of the first visible efforts on the part of the State Department of Education to make clear its support for inclusive practices.

In both examples, the work of CISP was outcome oriented, iterative, context specific, participatory, and explicit. The change process was dynamic and allowed for adjustment and change in either the policy (in the case of State A) or the implementation of the policy (in the case of State B).

Conclusion and Recommendations

The CISP approach to change was effective in addressing policy as well as implementation issues. The process helped state and local districts identify barriers to supporting inclusion and to identify why the barriers existed. The feedback process provided constituents and policymakers with opportunities to be heard and a venue for workable solutions to be developed through professional development efforts at all levels of the system.

Communication was a key aspect of the change strategy. Planned communication took place over an extended period within and across levels of the system. CISP issued specific invitations to stakeholders to participate in the feedback events rather than extending broad open invitations to groups, which we think helped promote participation. Frequent and recurring discussion tended to breed trust among the various stakeholders and lead to compromises and shared vision that supported the policy development and implementation process within and across levels of the system. Communication was fostered in a mixture of large and small venues. This allowed participants opportunities to disclose in settings where they felt their voices would be heard, or alternatively, in larger settings where anonymity was preferred. Ensuring that those who were providing feedback were free from retribution was critical to receiving honest feedback about existing policies and practices.

The statewide changes that took place have persisted since CISP completed its work in these states. CISP was not the sole cause of the changes described. Rather, CISP contributed to policy and practice shifts. CISP contributed to changes in the policy and practices through a bottom-up, context-specific process that enhanced knowledge and skills and addressed the expectations, beliefs, and relationships that affected the implementation of public policy at the state, district, and school levels. CISP contributed to the resolution of barriers to systemic change by facilitating problem-based communication within and across levels of the state education system.

Other reformers attempting this type of work may wish to carefully consider how to assemble a set of players who are in a position to actually make the types of decisions about which they are seeking resolution. Bringing diverse perspectives to the table enriches the conversations and strengthens the solutions that result from these deliberations. Technical assistance providers should be willing to broker support and assistance for schools and local districts as needed, rather than assuming all of the expertise will reside in their project team. Embedded professional development, delivered over an extended period of time, is critical in helping large systems change in substantive ways. "Drive-by/drop-in" episodic technical assistance is less expensive and less time intensive; however, it does not allow for differences in the culture/context, or for understanding the underlying causes of issues in the states and districts. Embedded, context-specific approaches at all levels of the system are needed to move conversations to a deeper level, and in the process, serve as a foundation for the relationships that are needed to reeducate personnel and change systems. Although we had some general parameters for our approach, it is important to point out that above all, we remained flexible and responsive to the changing needs and priorities of the districts and states with whom we worked. CISP worked in these states for a total of 4 years. Building trust takes time, but we found it was time well spent in our efforts to promote inclusive policies and practices on a large scale.

Finally, it is important to note that despite the inception of our work a decade ago, the issues that prompted the need for our capacity-building project remain as obstacles to the implementation of federally mandated general and special education policies (No Child Left Behind Act of 2001; Individuals With Disabilities Education Improvement Act of 2004) today. When teachers, principals, and other educators understand the connection between their work and the federal, state, and local policies that guide their work, they are better able to provide feedback to policymakers to get policies changed. Indeed, policymakers are often looking for the type of feedback teachers and principals provided through this project. We hope that the information in this article will be useful to others serving as agents of change and that more teachers and principals will see themselves as potential change agents in the future.

Acknowledgments

Data used to develop this article were gathered by CISP through a cooperative agreement (H324K980001A) awarded by the U.S. Department of Education, Office of Special Education Programs, to the Erikson Institute, Chicago, Illinois, Christine Salisbury, principal investigator. No official endorsement of the content is implied. The authors gratefully acknowledge the contributions of our CISP, state, and district colleagues, and our project officer, Dr. Anne Smith.

References

Bodilly, S. (1998). *Lessons from the new American schools' scale-up phase: Prospects for bringing designs to multiple schools.* Santa Monica, CA: Rand.

Bowen, M. L., & Klass, P. H. (1993). Low-incidence special education teacher preparation: A supply and capacity pilot study. *Teacher Education and Special Education, 16,* 248–257.

Buswell, B. E., Schaffner, C. B., & Seyler, A. B. (1999). *Opening doors: Connecting students to curriculum, classmates, and learning* (2nd ed.). Colorado Springs, CO: PEAK Parent Center.

Chin, R., & Benne, K. D. (1985). General strategies for effecting changes in human systems. In W. G. Bennis, K. D. Benne, & R. Chin (Eds.), *From the planning of change* (pp. 22–45). New York: Holt, Rhinehart, & Winston.

Deal, T. E. (1990). Reframing reform. *Educational Leadership, 48*(8): 6–9, 11–12.

Dirkx, J. M., Blodgett, C. S., & Turner, M. K. (n.d.). *Back to the future: Reflections on a commitment to change (CTC) strategy implemented in adult basic education practice.* Retrieved March 15, 2005, from http://literacy.kent.edu/~nebraska/research/future.html

Education of All Handicapped Children Act. of 1975, Pub. L. 94-142, 89 Stat. 773 (1975).

Fisher, D., & Frey, N. (2001). Access to the core curriculum: Critical ingredients for student success. *Remedial and Special Education, 22,* 148–157.

Fullan, M. (1993). *Change forces.* London: Falmer.

Fullan, M., & Miles, M. (1992). Getting reform right. What works and what doesn't. *Phi Delta Kappan, 73,* 744–752.

Fuhrman, S. (1993). The politics of coherence. *Designing coherent education policy: Improving the system.* San Francisco, CA: Jossey-Bass.

Gersten, R., & Brengelman, S. (1996). The quest to translate research into classroom practices: The emerging knowledge base. *Remedial and special education, 17*(2): 67–74.

Individuals With Disabilities Education Improvement Act of 2004, Pub. L. No. 108-446, 118 Stat. 2647 (2004).

Kronley, R. A., & Handley, C. (2001). *Framing the field: Professional development in context.* Washington, DC: The Finance Project.

Marks, A. C., & Wright, R. J. (2002, February). *Defining intrinsic and extrinsic motivators for continuing professional education.* Paper presented at the Annual Meeting of the Eastern Educational Research Association, Sarasota, FL.

McDonnell, L., & McLaughlin, M. J. (1997). *Educating one and all: Students with disabilities and standards-based reform.* Washington, DC: National Academies Press.

McGregor, G., & Vogelsberg, R. T. (1998). *Inclusive schooling practices: Pedagogical and research foundations.* Baltimore: Brookes/Consortium on Inclusive Schooling Practices.

McLaughlin, M. J., Henderson, K., & Rhim, L. (1998). *Snapshots of reform: How five local districts are interpreting standards-based reform for students with disabilities.* Alexandria, VA: National Association of State Boards of Education.

Moscovitch, E. (1993). *Special education: Good intentions gone awry.* Boston: Pioneer Institute for Public Policy Research.

National Association of State Boards of Education (1992). *Winners all: A call for inclusive schools.* Alexandria, VA: Author.

No Child Left Behind Act of 2001, Pub. L. No. 107-110, 115 Stat. 1425 (2002). Retrieved January 14, 2005, from http://www.ed.gov/policy/elsec/leg/esea02/index.html

Roach, V., Ashcroft, J., & Stamp, A. (1995). In D. Kysilko, (Ed.), *Winning ways: Creating inclusive schools, classrooms and communities.* Alexandria, VA: National Association of State Boards of Education.

Salisbury, C., Strieker, T., Roach, V., & McGregor, G. (2001). *Pathways to inclusive practices: Systems oriented, policy-linked, and research-based strategies that work.* Chicago: Erikson Institute/Consortium on Inclusive School Practices.

Sands, D. J., Kozelski, E. B., & French, N. K. (2000). *Inclusive education for the 21st century.* Belmont, CA: Wadsworth.

Sargent, T. A. (2000). *Linking educators' professional development to workplace/community learning experiences.* Madison: University of Wisconsin–Madison, Center on Education and Work.

Skrtic, T. M. (1991). *Behind special education: A critical analysis of professional culture and school organization.* Denver, CO: Love.

Smith, M., & O'Day, J. (1991). Systemic school reform. In S. H. Fuhrman & B. Malden. (Eds.), *The politics of curriculum and testing, 1990 yearbook of the politics of education association* (pp. 233–267). Washington, DC: Falmer.

Villa, R., & Thousand, J. (1995). *Creating an inclusive school.* Alexandria, VA: Association for Supervision and Curriculum Development.

Villa, R., & Thousand, J. (Eds.). (2000). *Restructuring for caring and effective education: Putting the puzzle together* (2nd ed.). Baltimore: Brookes.

Wang, M. C., Reynolds, M. C., & Walberg, H. J. (1988). Integrating the children of the second system. *Phi Delta Kappan, 70,* 248–251.

Additional Resources for Classroom Use

Frey, The Role of 1:1 Individual Instruction in Reading (pp. 207–214)

1. Frey, N., & Fisher, D. (2004). The role of the literacy professional in addressing the disproportionate representation of culturally and linguistically diverse students in special education. In D. Lapp, C. C. Block, E. J. Cooper, J. Flood, N. Roser & J. V. Tinajero (Eds.), *Teaching all the children: Strategies for developing literacy in an urban setting* (pp. 231–254). New York: Guilford.

This chapter, from the *Solving Problems in the Teaching of Literacy* series, outlines how literacy professionals such as reading specialists and literacy coaches can play an active role in supporting the learning of students with individualized education plans. Oral language development, listening, reading, and writing skills are addressed.

2. Honig, B., Diamond, L., & Gutlohn, L. (2000). *Teaching reading sourcebook for kindergarten through eighth grade.* Novato, CA: Arena.

An outstanding source for teachers working with students reading at levels different from the rest of the class. This sourcebook offers an array of instructional approaches for developing students' phonemic awareness, decoding, spelling, vocabulary, and comprehension abilities. Although daunting in size, the book is formatted for finding information quickly.

3. Shanker, J. L., & Ekwall, E. E. (2003). *Locating and correcting reading difficulties* (8th ed.). Upper Saddle River, NJ: Merrill Prentice Hall.

This useful tool offers a comprehensive set of tools for diagnosing specific reading difficulties, including emergent reading, decoding skills, oral reading, comprehension, and study skills. The perforated pages make it easy to duplicate the instruments for use with students. In addition, each reading difficulty is accompanied by a thorough discussion of instructional lessons to address the skills and strategies.

Janney and Snell, Modifying Schoolwork in Inclusive Classrooms (pp. 215–223)

1. McNary, S. J., Glasgow, N. A., & Hicks, C. D. (2005). *What successful teachers do in inclusive classrooms.* Thousand Oaks, CA: Corwin Press.

This user-friendly compendium of 60 research-based teaching strategies gives brief syntheses of relevant research, specific application tactics, and sources for further reading.

2. National Information Center for Children and Youth With Disabilities Web site

   http://www.nichcy.org

   This Web site offers a wide array of fact sheets, news digests, research briefs, and resource lists on topics such as disability classifications, special education law, individualized education plan requirements, and inclusion strategies.

3. Mastropieri, M. A., & Scruggs, T. E. (2000). *The inclusive classroom: Strategies for effective instruction.* Columbus, OH: Merrill.

   This rich and helpful book provides descriptions and illustrative examples of instructional practices that have been proven to be effective for a wide range of students with and without disabilities. Topics range from visual strategies and strategic teaching to cooperative learning and peer tutoring.

Bond and Castagnera, Peer Supports and Inclusive Education: An Underutilized Resource (pp. 224–229)

1. Keefe, E. B., Moore, V. M., & Duff, F. R. (2006). *Listening to the experts: Students with disabilities speak out.* Baltimore: Brookes.

   This unique book offers the reader a candid look at what really works for students with disabilities—from the perspective of the students themselves. Students with varying degrees of disability speak of their school experiences in both self-contained classrooms and inclusive classrooms. Specific strategies that students and professionals have found useful are highlighted, such as peer supports and coteaching.

French and Chopra, Teachers as Executives (pp. 230–238)

1. The PAR²A Center Web site

   http://www.paracenter.org

   This site offers information for paraeducators as well as a forum where paraeducators can interact with others across the country. For teachers who supervise paraeducators there is a special section that provides worksheets as well as ideas to enrich their skills. For administrators or staff developers looking for training models and materials, the Comprehensive Training Opportunities for Paraeducators Paraeducator Training program is described. The calendar feature shows key events that are of interest to those who supervise or train paraeducators, and the latest news feature keeps the visitor abreast of the latest happenings in the world of paraeducators.

2. Special Connections Web site

   http://www.specialconnections.ku.edu

   This site offers a wealth of strategies on topics of instruction, assessment, collaboration, and behavior. Each section includes case studies and opportunities to interact with the information. The section on collaboration features coteaching and paraeducator supervision. The paraeducator supervision section offers a multitude of tools and examples for teachers who want to improve their skills in this area.

3. Paraeducator and Supervisor Training Designed to Meet the Needs of Students With Disabilities in General Education Classrooms Web site

   http://www.uvm.edu/~cdci/paraprep

   This site provides information about a range of topics, including acknowledging paraeducators; orienting and training paraeducators, hiring and assigning paraeducators, paraeducator interactions with students and staff, roles and responsibilities of paraeducators, and supervision and evaluation of paraeducator services. It also contains a list of references to print materials and other Web sites.

Thousand, Villa, and Nevin, The Many Faces of Collaborative Planning and Teaching (pp. 239–248)

1. Hourcade, J., & Bauwens, J. (2002). *Cooperative teaching: Re-building and sharing the schoolhouse.* Austin, TX: Pro-Ed.

This is a practical presentation of how elementary and secondary teachers can work together to better serve all the students in their classrooms. Different ways of structuring co-teaching are emphasized with general and special educators varying their direct instruction roles.

2. Pugach, M. C., & Johnson, I. J. (2002). *Collaborative practitioners, collaborative schools* (2nd ed.). Denver, CO: Love.

This is a helpful resource on how professionals and families might work together on school-based teams. The focus is on turning theory into practice.

Browder, Wakeman, and Flowers, Assessment of Progress in the General Curriculum for Students With Disabilities (pp. 249–259)

1. Center for Applied Special Technology (CAST) – National Center on Accessing the General Curriculum Web site

   http://www.cast.org/policy/ncac/index.html

   In a collaborative agreement with the U.S. Department of Education's Office of Special Programs, CAST established the National Center on Accessing the General Curriculum (NCAC) to provide a vision of how new curricula, teaching practices, and policies can be woven together to create practical approaches for improved access to the general curriculum by students with disabilities. To help educators do this, NCAC researchers and partners have produced a number of publications. They are organized into the following categories: curriculum, teacher practice, policy, and consensus building. The publications are available as HTML pages, Microsoft Word documents, and PDF documents. They may be reviewed and downloaded from the NCAC publications page.

2. The National Center on Student Progress Monitoring Web site

   http://www.studentprogress.org/

   To meet the challenges of implementing effective progress monitoring, the Office of Special Education Programs funded the National Center on Student Progress Monitoring. Housed at the American Institutes for Research, and working in conjunction with researchers from Vanderbilt University, the center is a national technical assistance and dissemination center dedicated to the implementation of scientifically based student progress monitoring. The Center's mission is to provide technical assistance to states and districts and disseminate information about progress monitoring practices proven to work in different academic content areas (Grades K–5). The Web site offers a library that includes articles and research, presentations, training, and frequently asked questions about progress monitoring. The site also has resources for parents and teachers about progress monitoring that are written in family-friendly language.

3. The National Center on Educational Outcomes Web site

   http://education.umn.edu/nceo/

   The National Center on Educational Outcomes (NCEO) provides national leadership in the participation of students with disabilities in national and state assessments, standards-setting efforts, and graduation requirements. NCEO performs many services, including working with states and federal agencies to identify important outcomes of education for students with disabilities; examining the participation of students in national and state assessments, including the use of accommodations and alternate assessments; and evaluating national and state practices in reporting assessment information on students with disabilities. The center provides reports on many topics.

Artiles, Harris-Murri, and Rostenberg, Inclusion as Social Justice: Critical Notes on Discourses, Assumptions, and the Road Ahead (pp. 260–268)

1. National Center for Culturally Responsive Educational Systems Web site

http://www.nccrest.org/

This project provides technical assistance and professional development to close the achievement gap between culturally and linguistically diverse students and their peers, and reduce inappropriate referrals to special education. Also included are publications, tools, research, and resources to assist families, teachers, principals, schools, and districts as they work to create culturally responsive programs in general and special education.

2. Berres, M. S., Ferguson, D. L., Knoblock, P., & Woods, C. (1996). *Creating tomorrow's schools today: Stories of inclusion, change, and renewal.* New York: Teachers College Press.

The authors discuss inclusion of children with disabilities in general education settings, and present accounts of successful inclusive school communities. Case studies on mainstreaming in education, special education, school management and organization, and educational change help readers see how schools can make equal academic efforts for all children.

3. Ferguson, D. K., Kozleski, E. B., & Smith, A. (2001). *Transformed, inclusive schools: A framework to guide fundamental change in urban schools.* On Point Series. National Institute for Urban School Improvement. Retrieved October 31, 2005, from the National Institute for Urban School Improvement Web site

http://www.urbanschools.org/pdf/TransformedSchools.pdf

The authors provide a framework for systemic change—developed by the National Institute for Urban School Improvement—to help transform noninclusive schools into schools that are inclusive and multicultural. The Systemic Change Framework is proposed as a useful tool that helps structure and network change efforts at district, school, and classroom levels to effect student achievement and learning.

McLeskey and Waldron, Comprehensive School Reform and Inclusive Schools (pp. 269–278)

1. Salend, S. (2005). *Creating inclusive classrooms: Effective and reflective practices for all students* (5th ed.). Upper Saddle River, NJ: Prentice Hall.

This book emphasizes developing an inclusive classroom that meets the needs of all students, regardless of disability, gender, socioeconomic status, family structure, ethnicity, or linguistic background. Student diversity in inclusive classrooms is presented and discussed in the context of effective classroom settings, practices, and instructional strategies. A wealth of information and ideas are provided for teachers across age levels and content areas.

2. Tomlinson, C. (2001). *How to differentiate instruction in mixed-ability classrooms.* Alexandria, VA: Association for Supervision and Curriculum Development.

This book provides strategies that teachers can use to create classrooms that support differentiated instruction. Tomlinson provides rich information regarding how teachers can use students' readiness levels, interests, and learning profiles to address student diversity. Strategies include curriculum compacting, "sidebar" investigations, entry points, graphic organizers, contracts, and portfolios.

Roach and Salisbury, Promoting Systemic, Statewide Inclusion From the Bottom Up (pp. 279–286)

1. Milligan, S., Fink, D., Delconte, V., Korenich, R., Salisbury, C., Anthony, L., et al. (2000). *Building level indicators of effective practices.* Retrieved October 15, 2005, from the National Institute for Urban School Improvement Web site

http://urbanschools.org/pdf/BLI_FINAL1.pdf

This self-assessment is designed to be used by school leaders to judge the effectiveness of their school in meeting the needs of all students. It is designed for those wishing to engage in whole-school reform and provides ratings in five key areas related to highly effective schools: instructional program, learning community, learning climate, organizational structure, and leadership. Users are advised that school leaders may be defined in a variety of ways, yet the final area, leadership, is to be completed by the building principal. This limitation reflects the project from which this self-assessment was developed (The Principal's Project) and can probably be disregarded. The assessment provides an excellent starting point for anyone seeking to make systemic changes toward inclusion in their school.

2. Strieker, T., Salisbury, C., & Roach, V. (2001). *Determining policy support for inclusive schools.* Retrieved October 15, 2005, from the National Institute for Urban School Improvement Web site

http://urbanschools.org/pdf/DPSFIS.pdf

This document complements the building-level self-assessment, *Building Level Indicators of Effective Practices,* by "help[ing] a planning team assess how inclusive their state and/or district policies are" (p. 2). The intended audiences for this assessment are policymakers, educators, and advocates who are interested in pinpointing policy barriers to inclusion, gaps between inclusive practice and policy, and the level of alignment of policy between state and local district policy. Underlying this self-assessment is the presumption that effective classroom practice cannot be sustained on a wide scale without supporting policies. Recognizing that change has to be prioritized based on the context, the tool also provides for a rating of the priority of each indicator for the team. The smallest unit of change for this assessment is the district.

For Product Safety Concerns and Information please contact our EU representative GPSR@taylorandfrancis.com
Taylor & Francis Verlag GmbH, Kaufingerstraße 24, 80331 München, Germany

www.ingramcontent.com/pod-product-compliance
Lightning Source LLC
Chambersburg PA
CBHW060517300426
44112CB00017B/2712